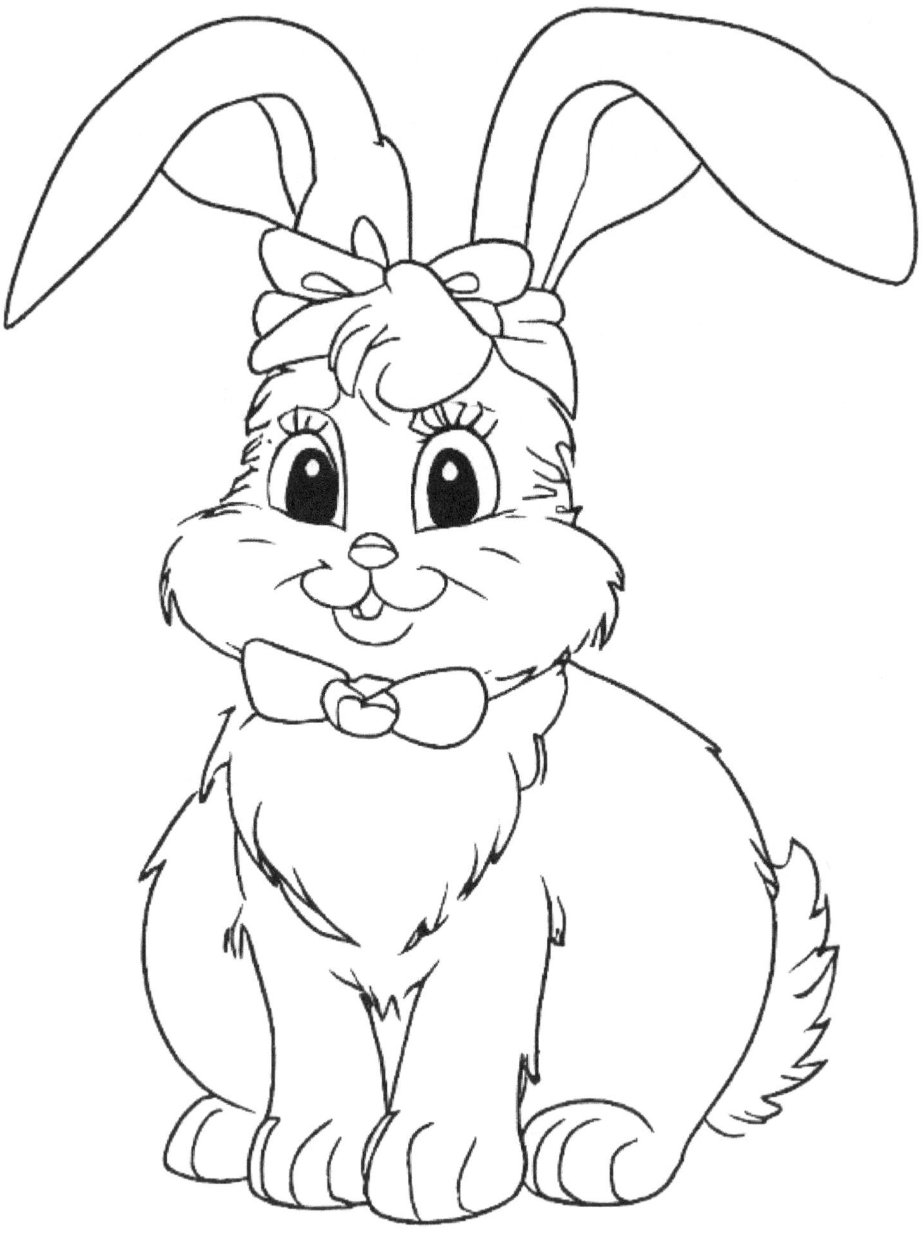

rabbit

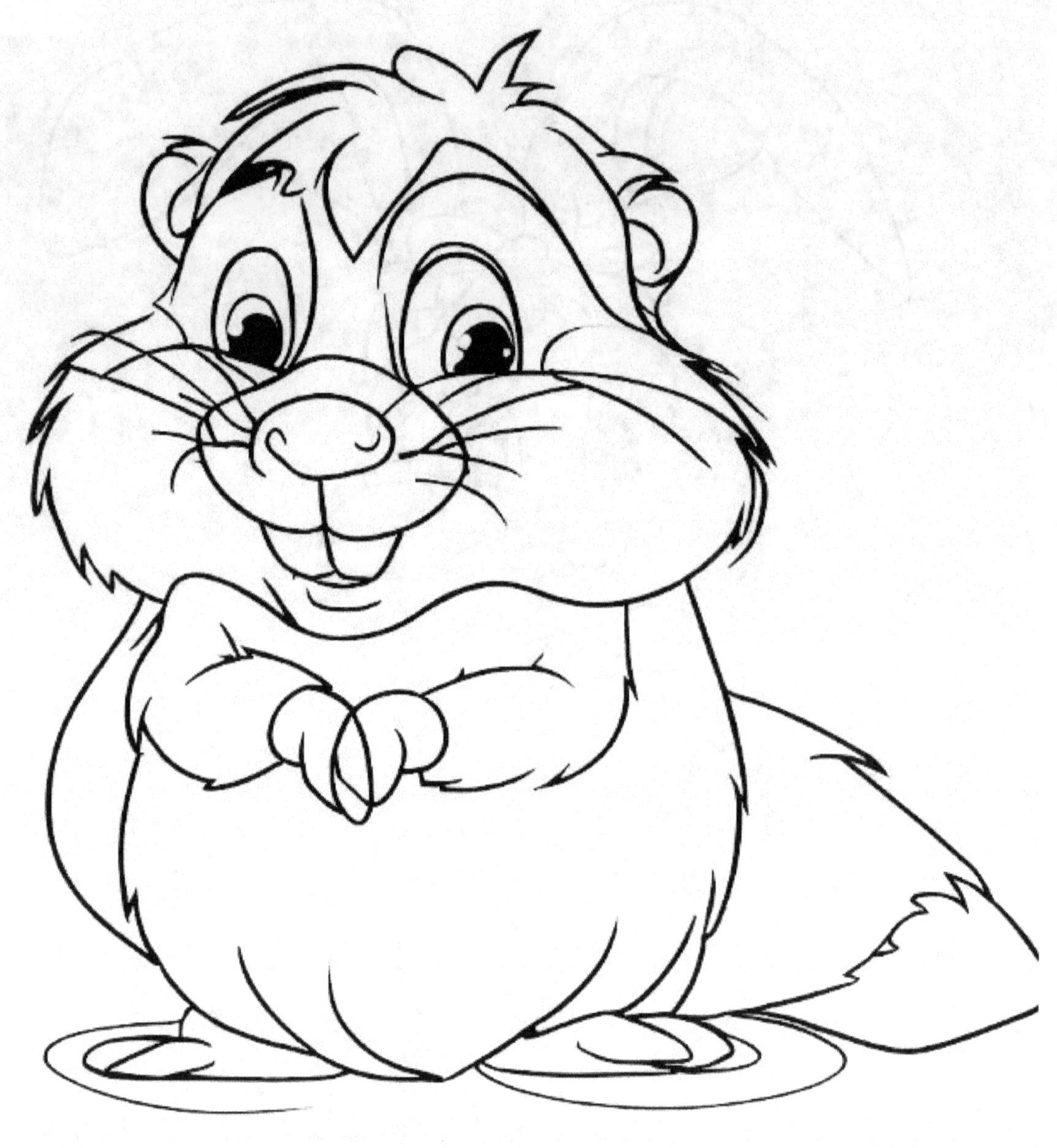

American
beaver

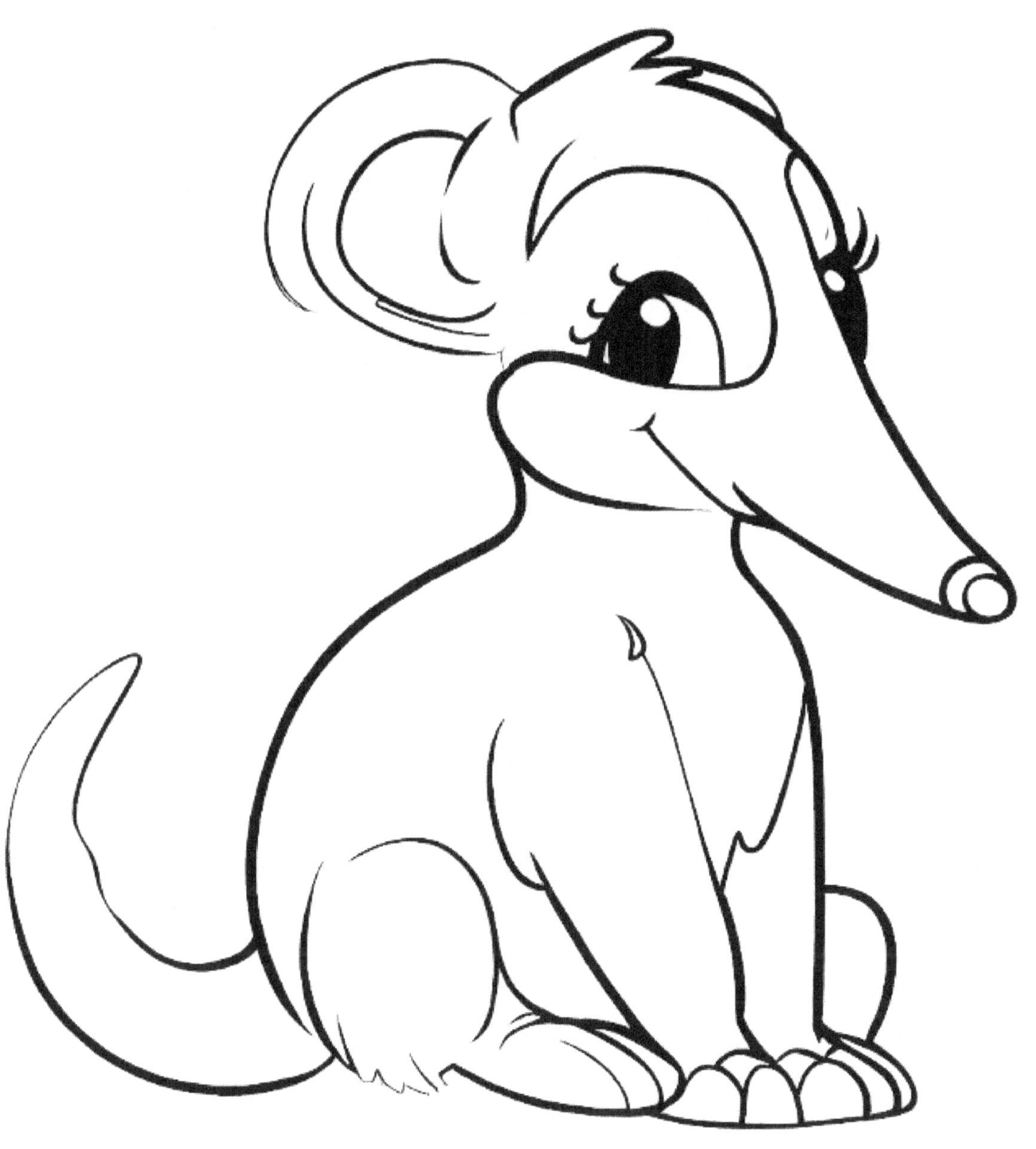

anteater

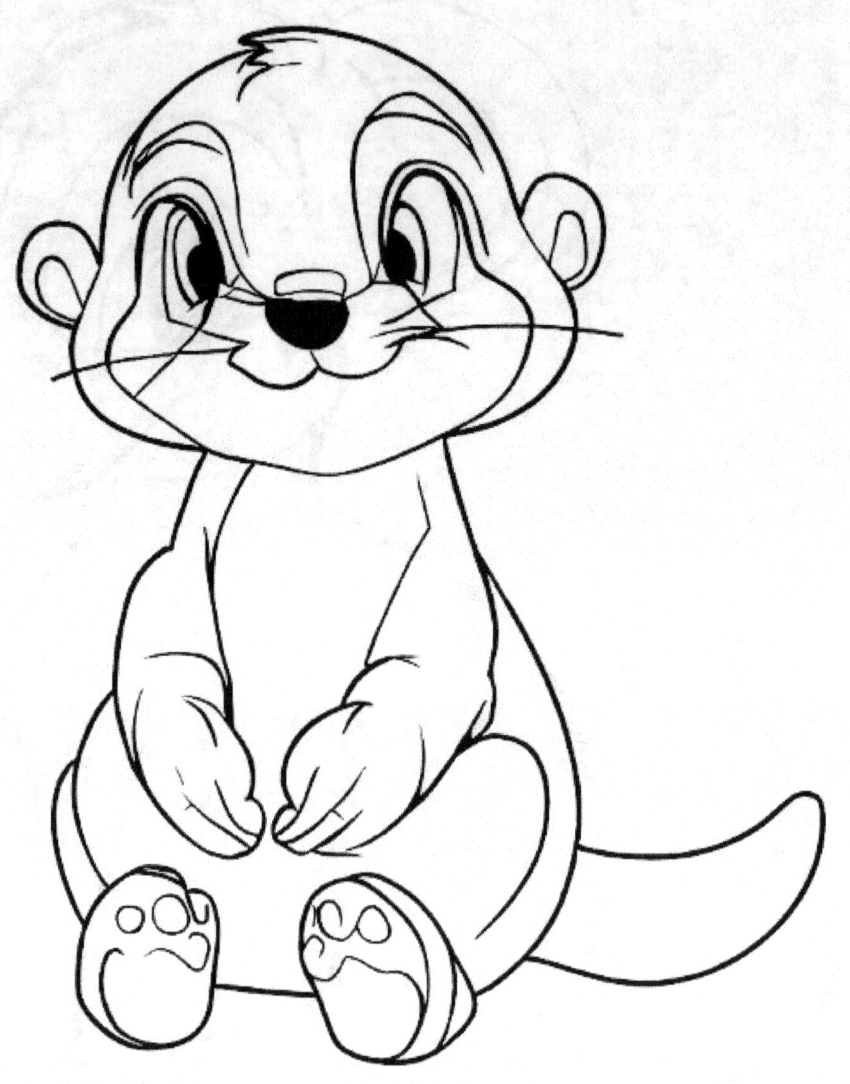

Baby otter

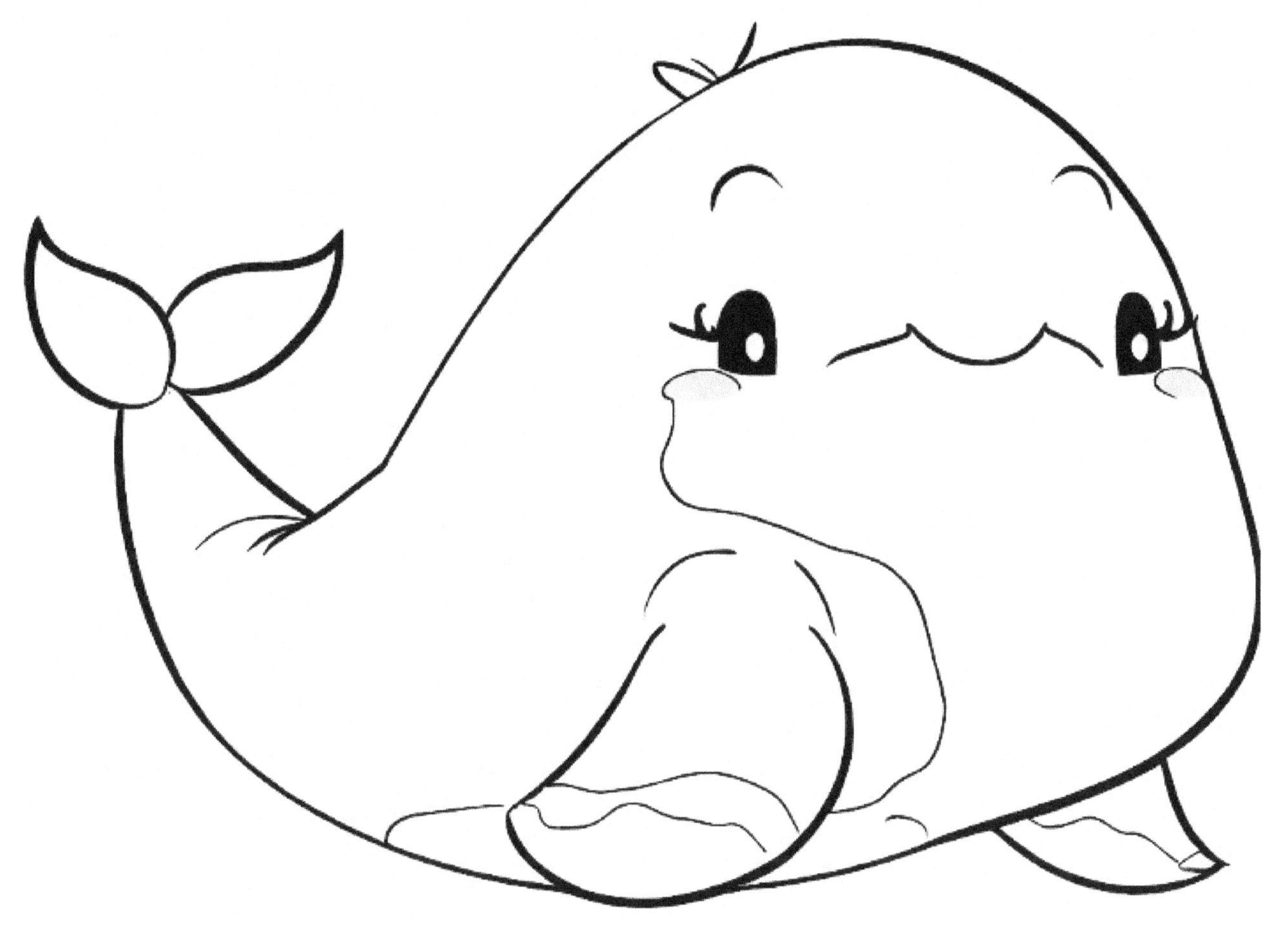

white
whale

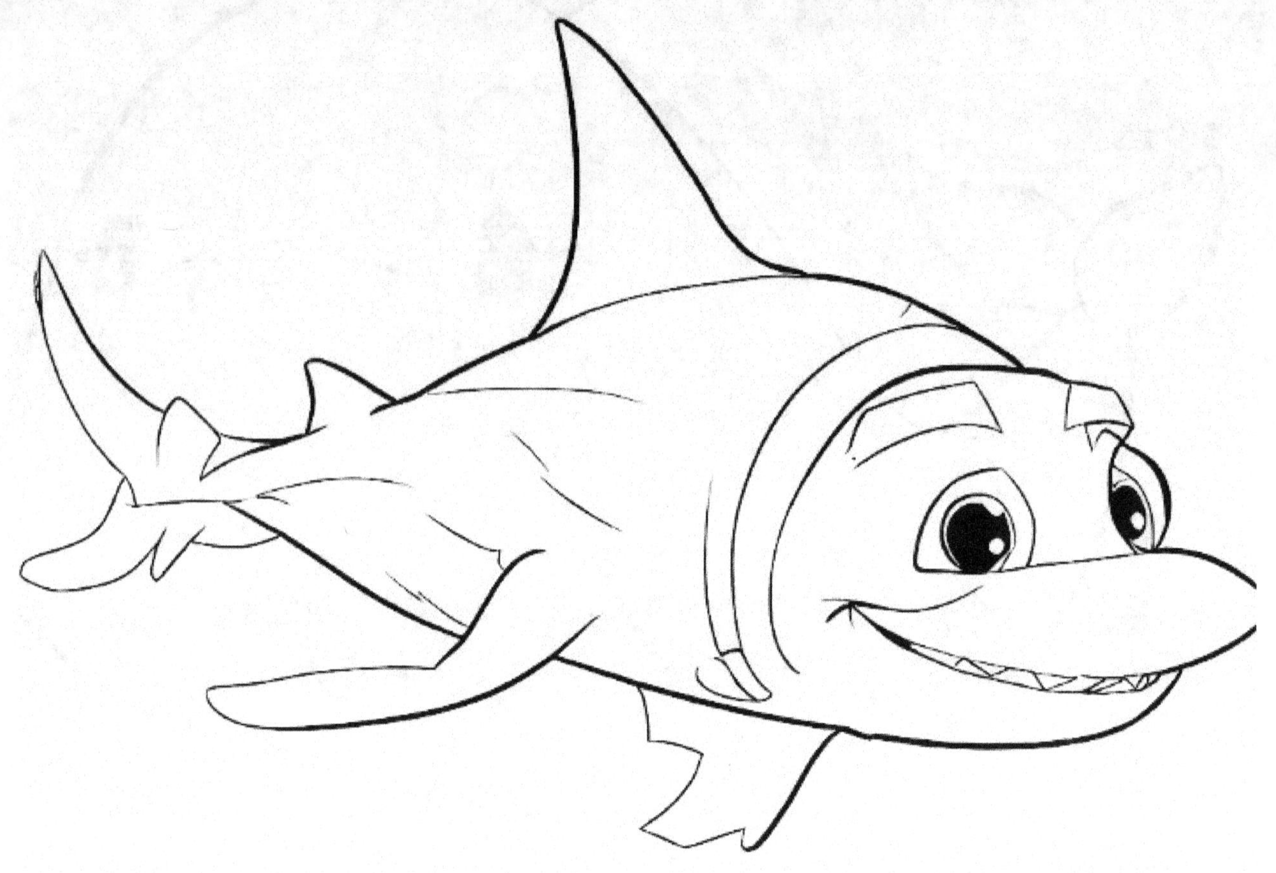

Bamboo shark

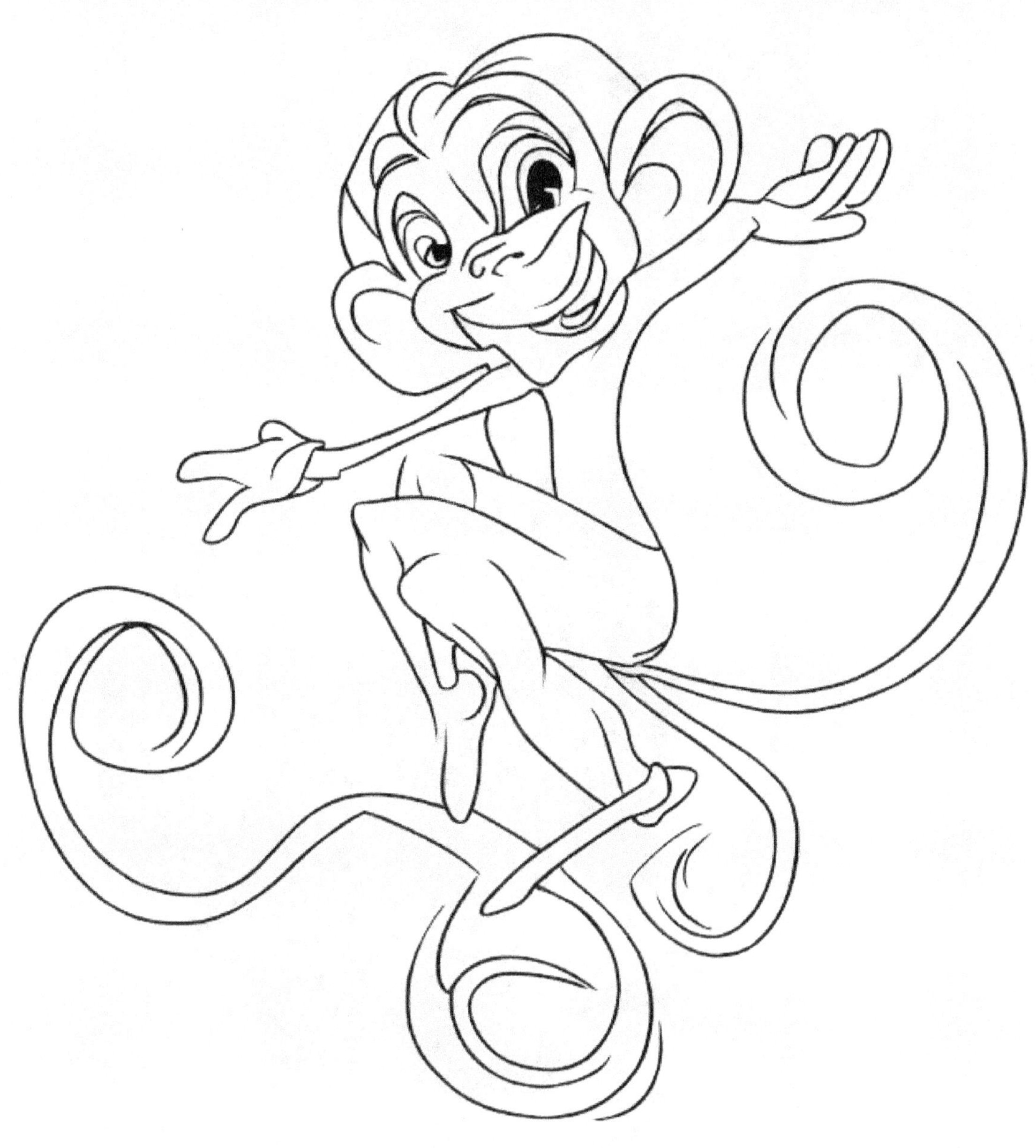

Big-nosed monkey

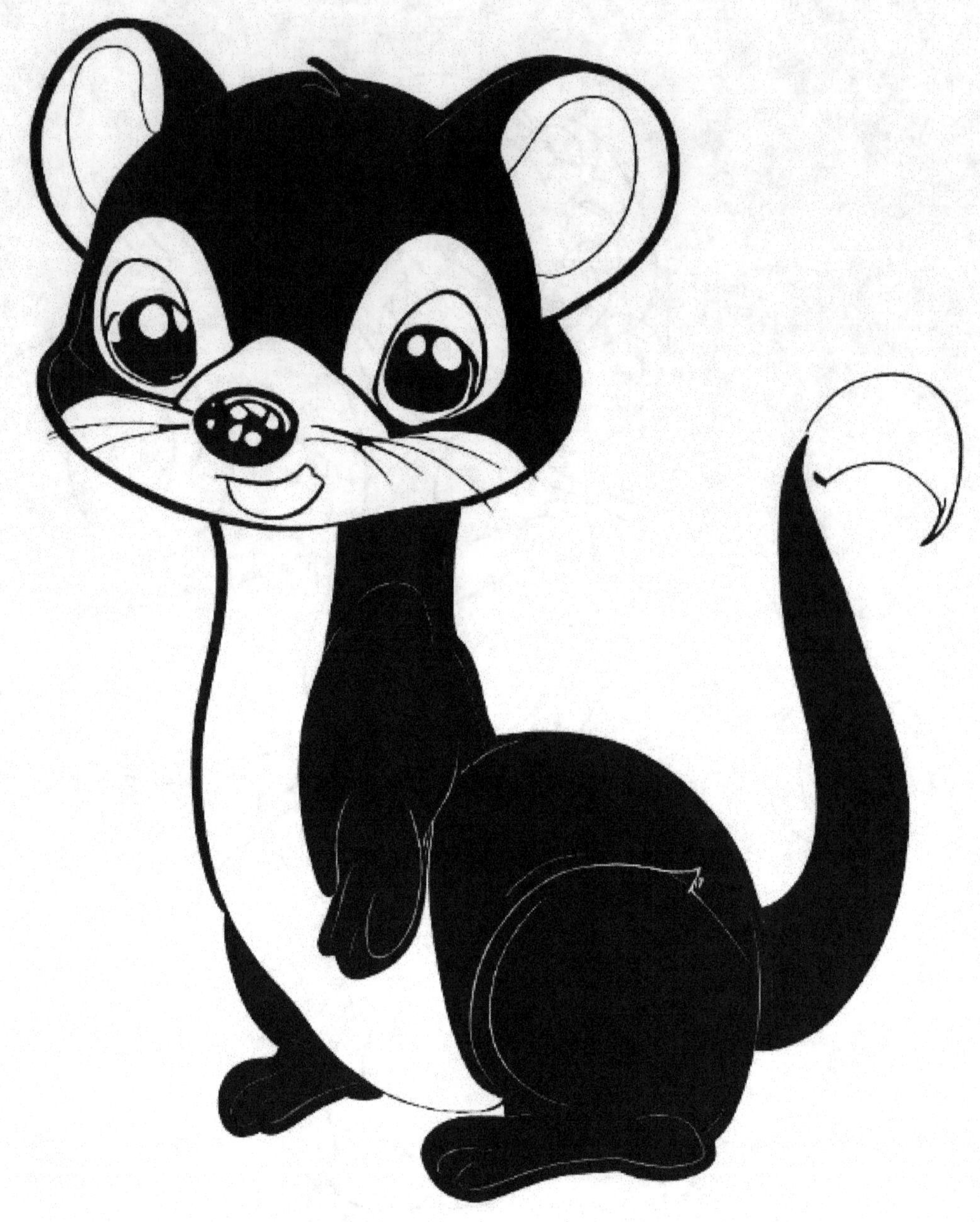

Black-footed Ferret

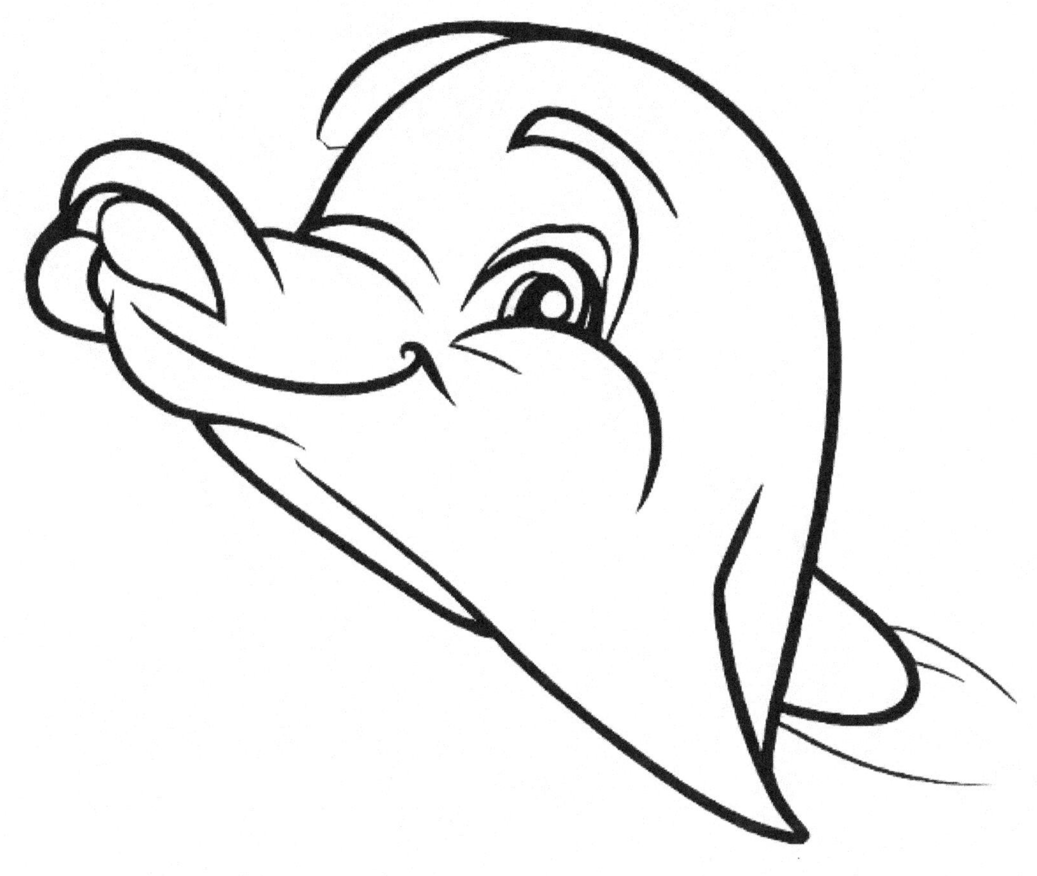

Bottlenose dolphin

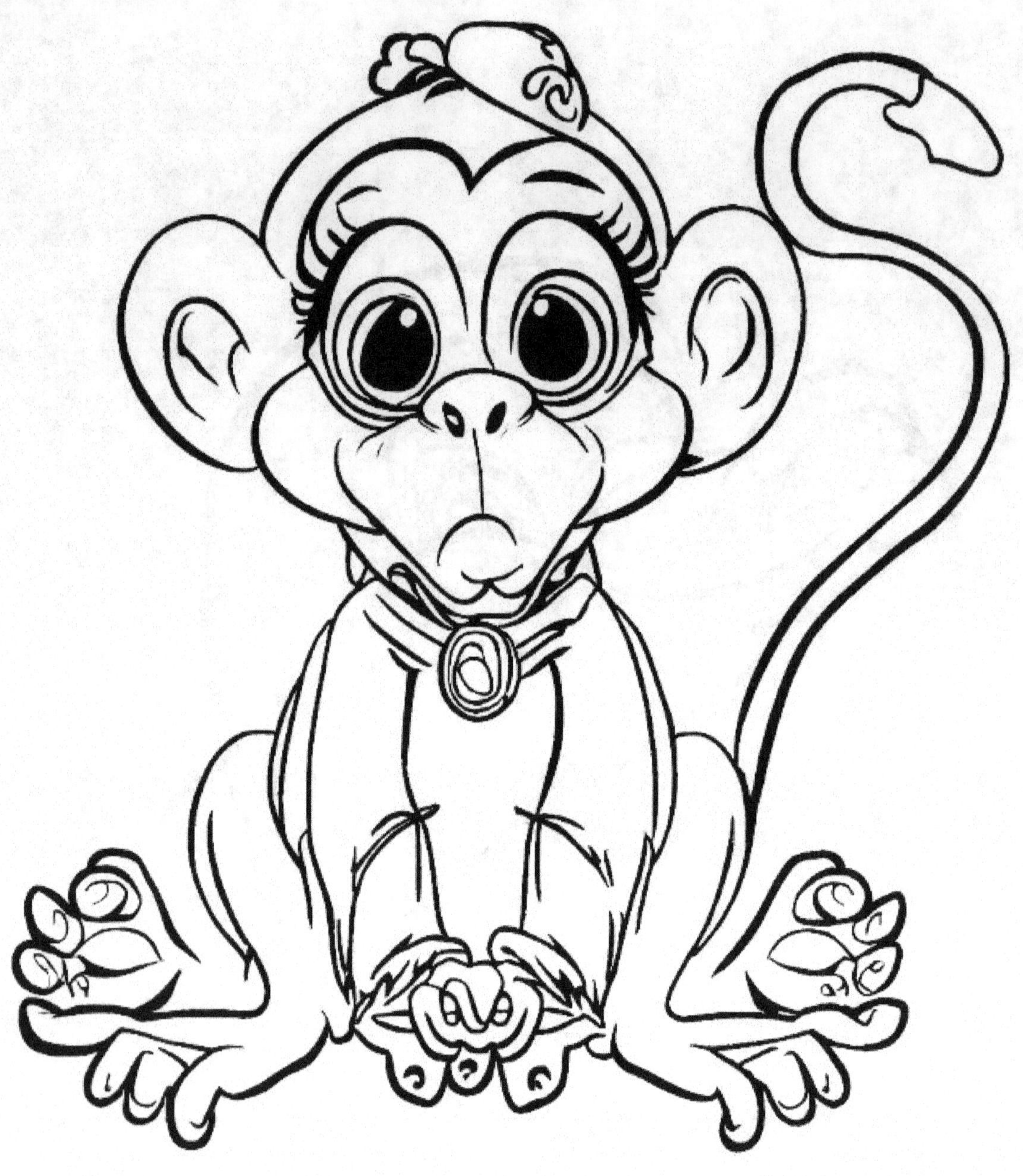

chimpanzee

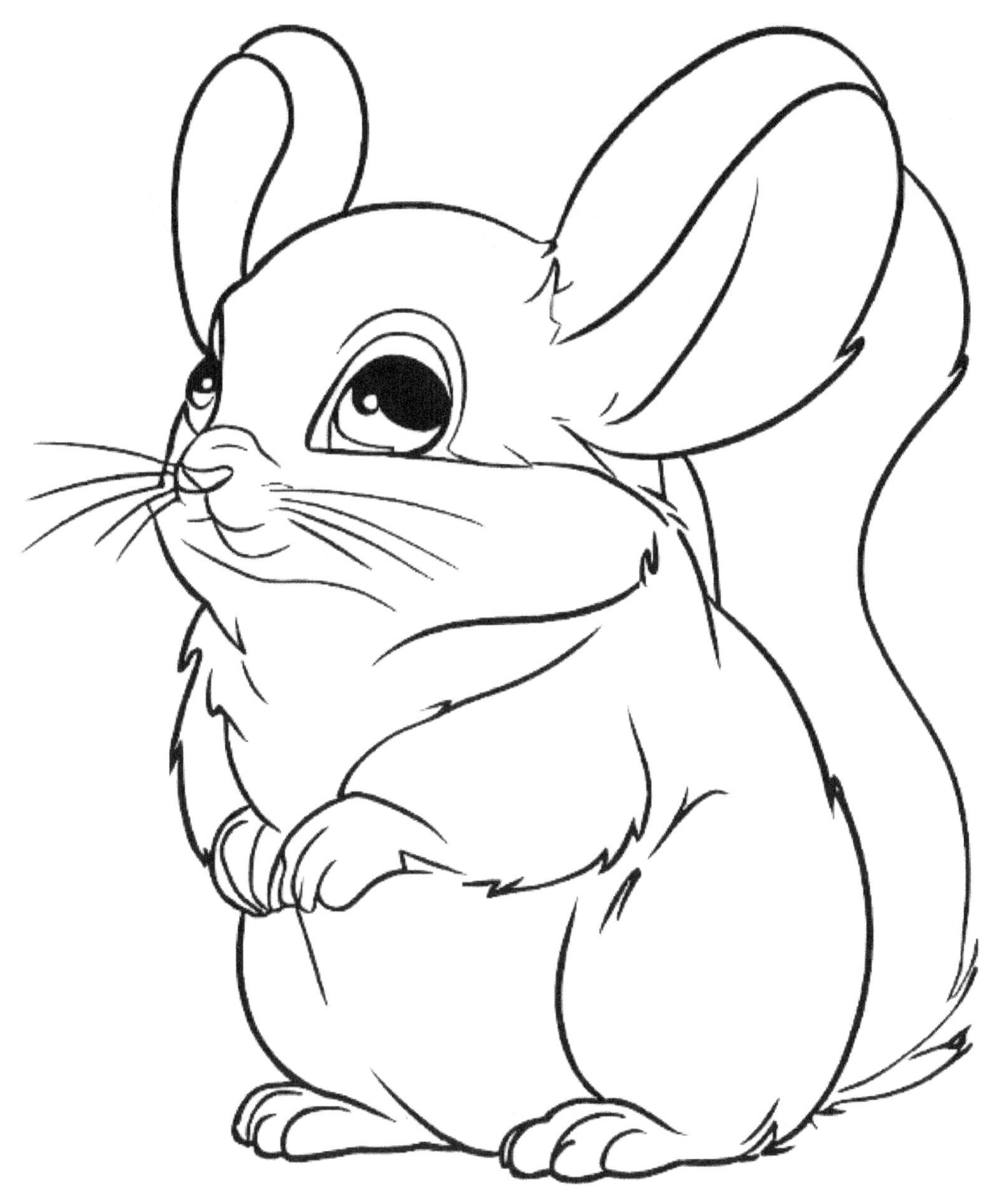

Common
Chinchilla

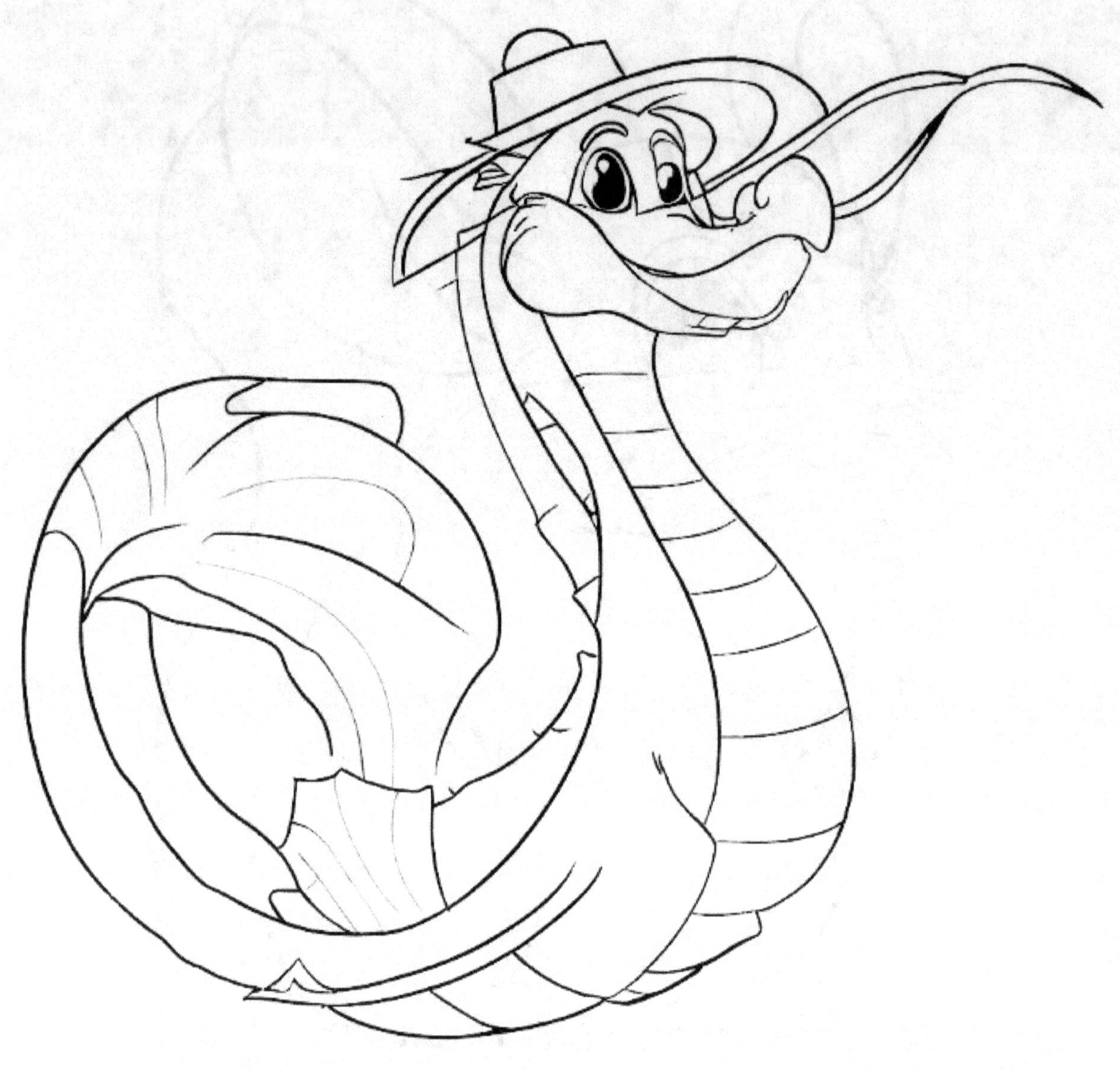

Common sea dragon

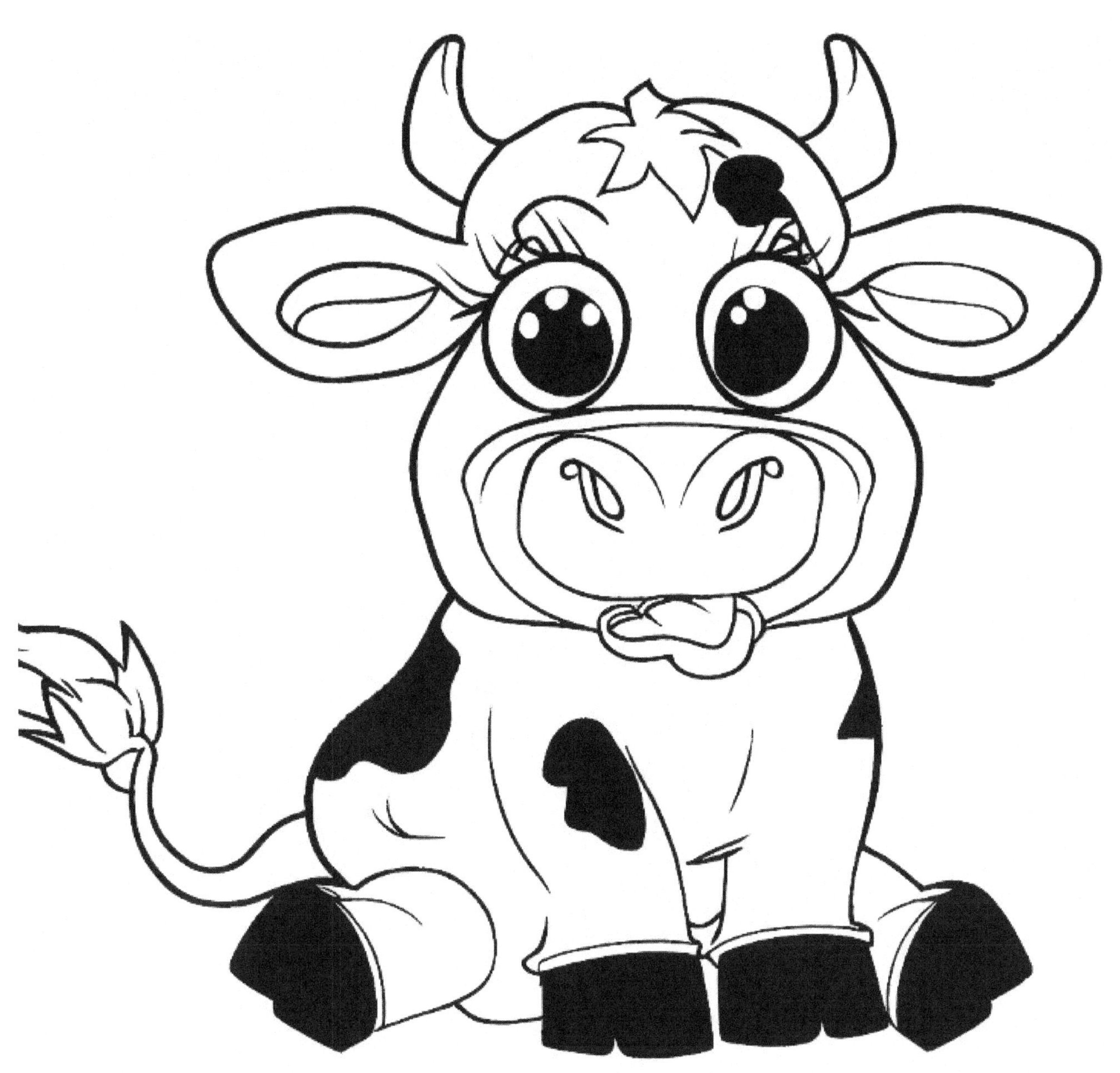

cow

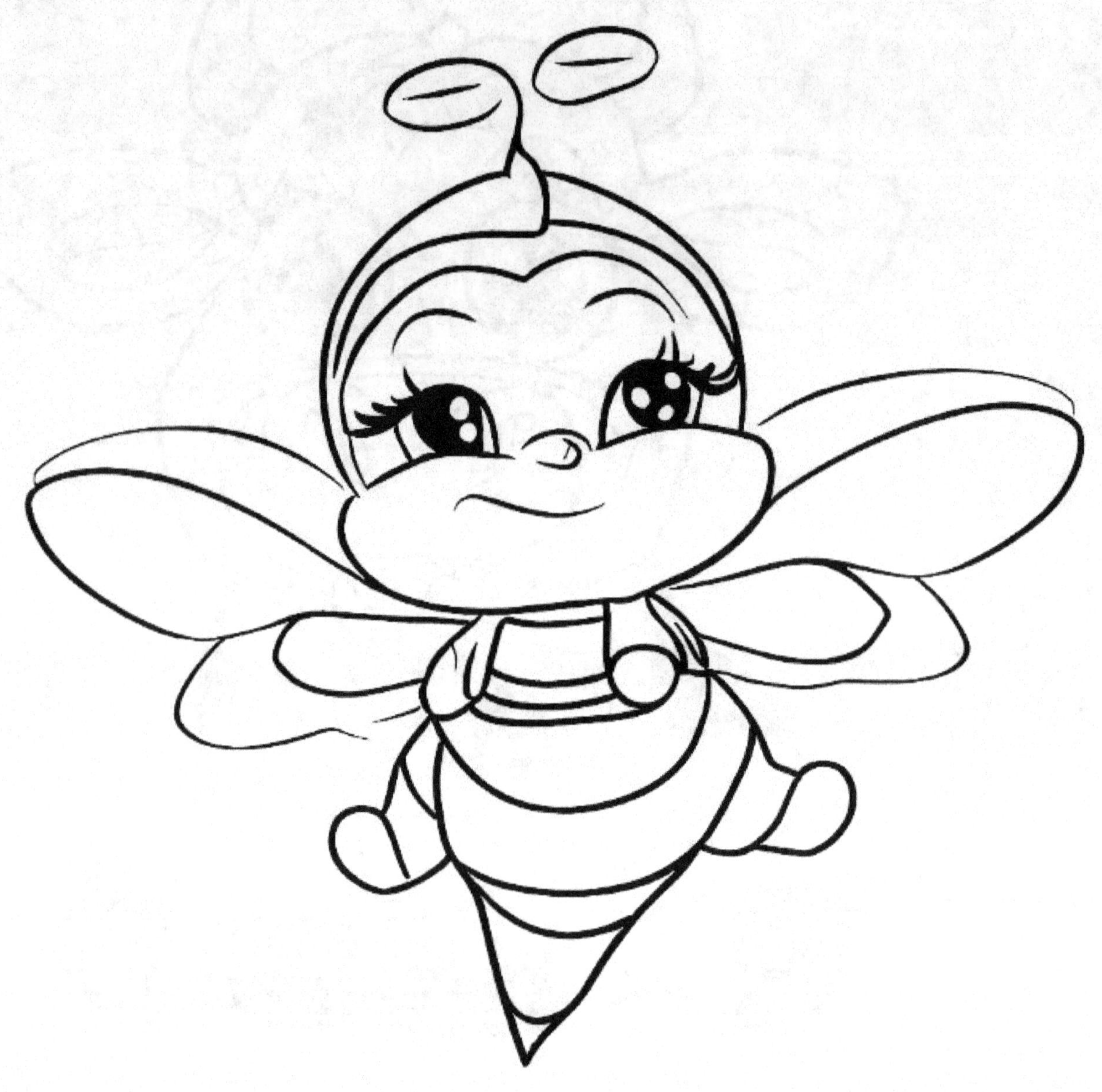

Cuban bee-
hummingbird

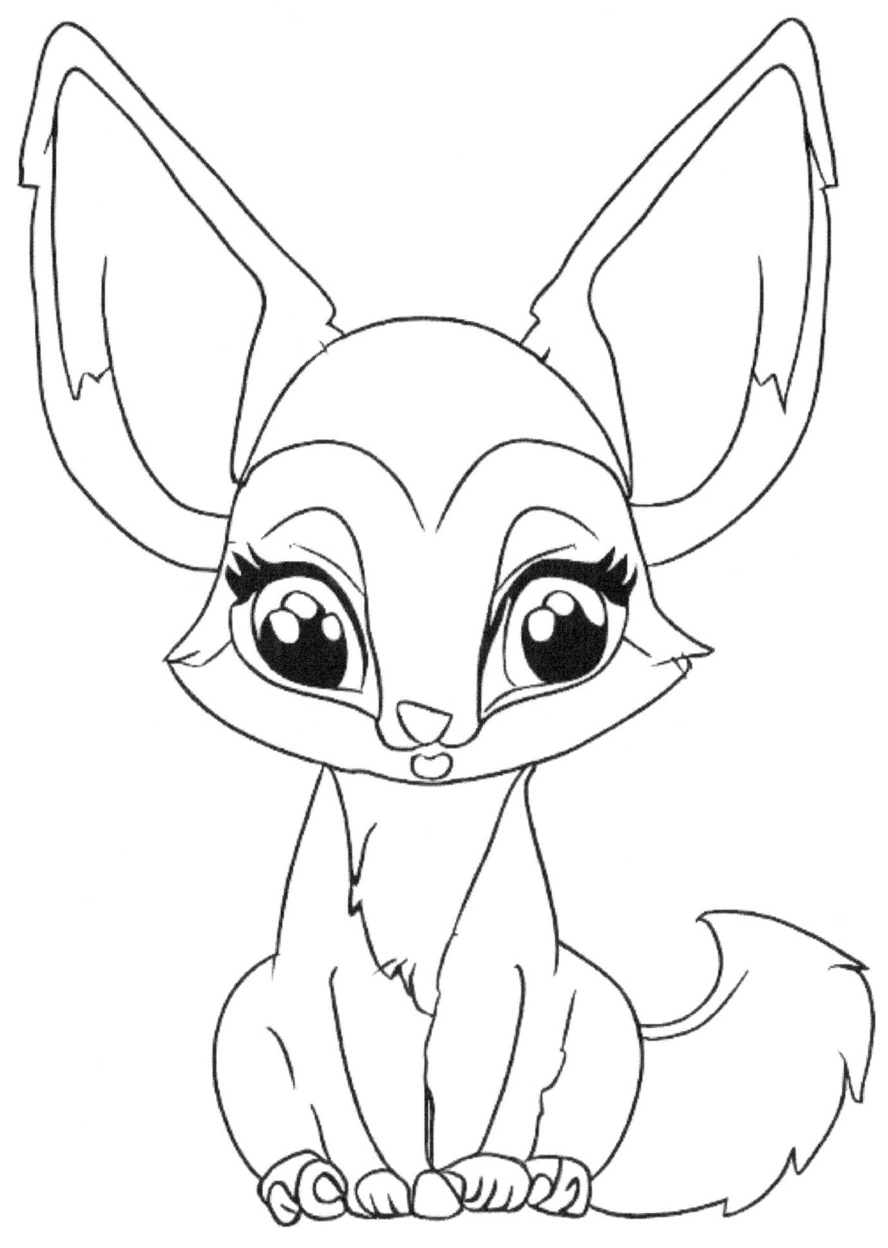

Desert Fox

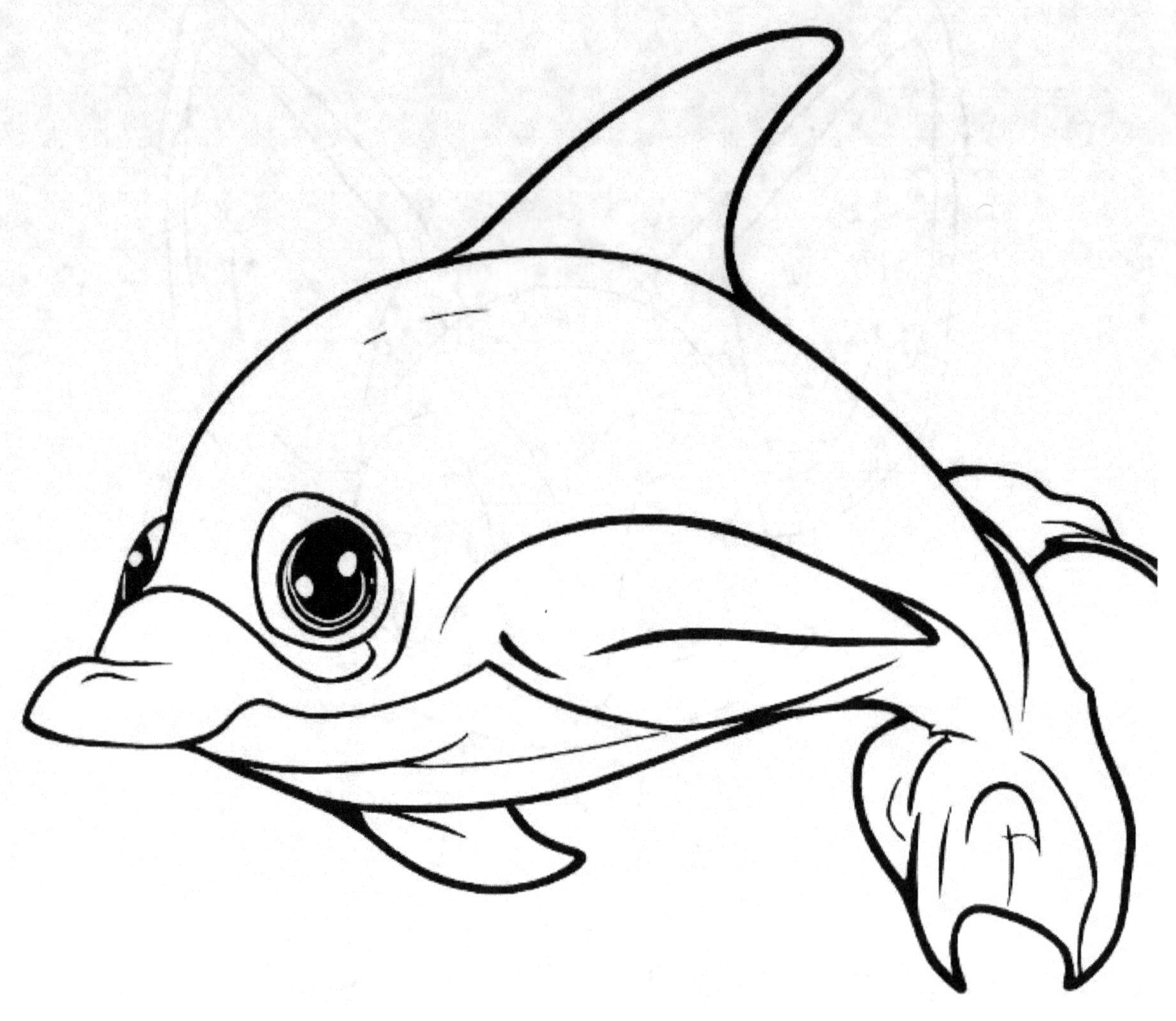

dolphin

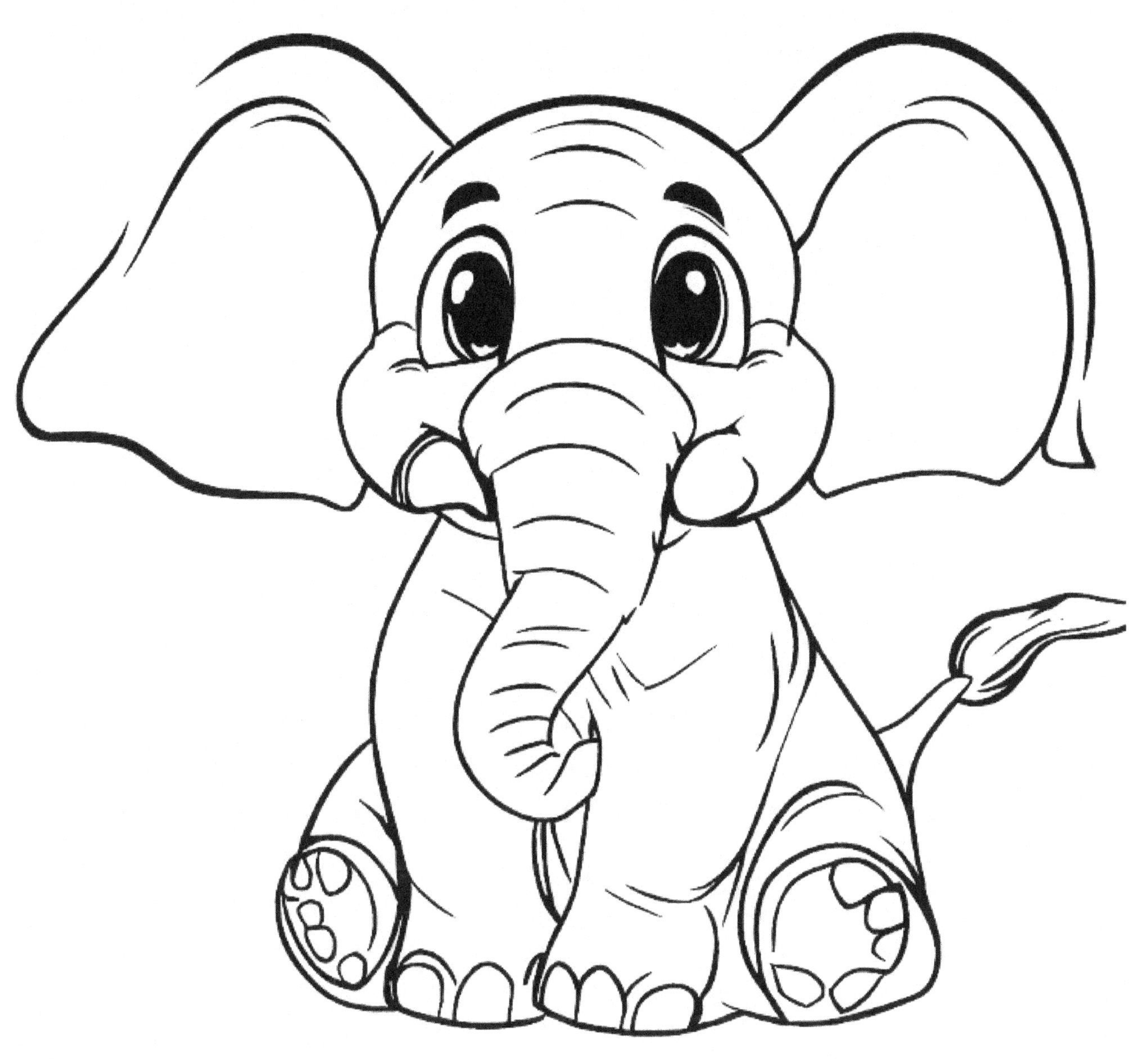

elephant

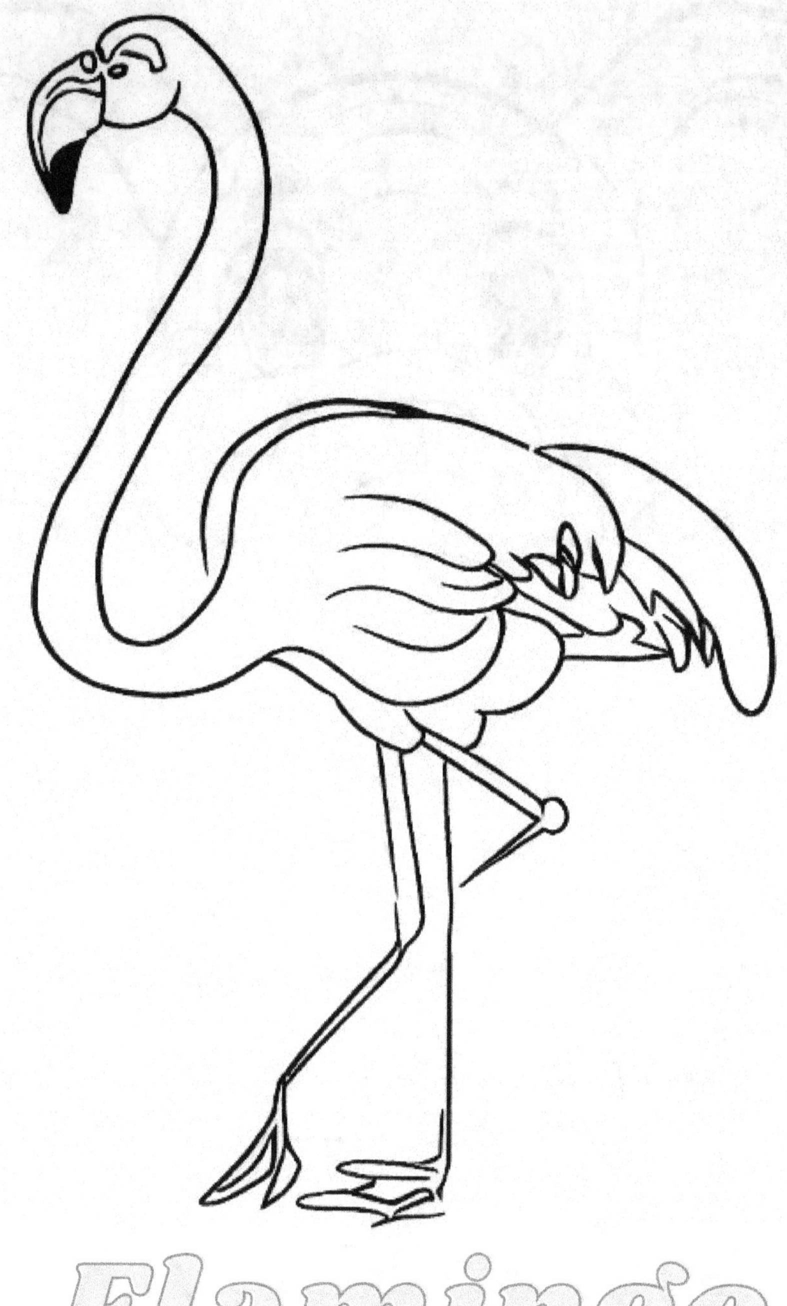
Flamingo

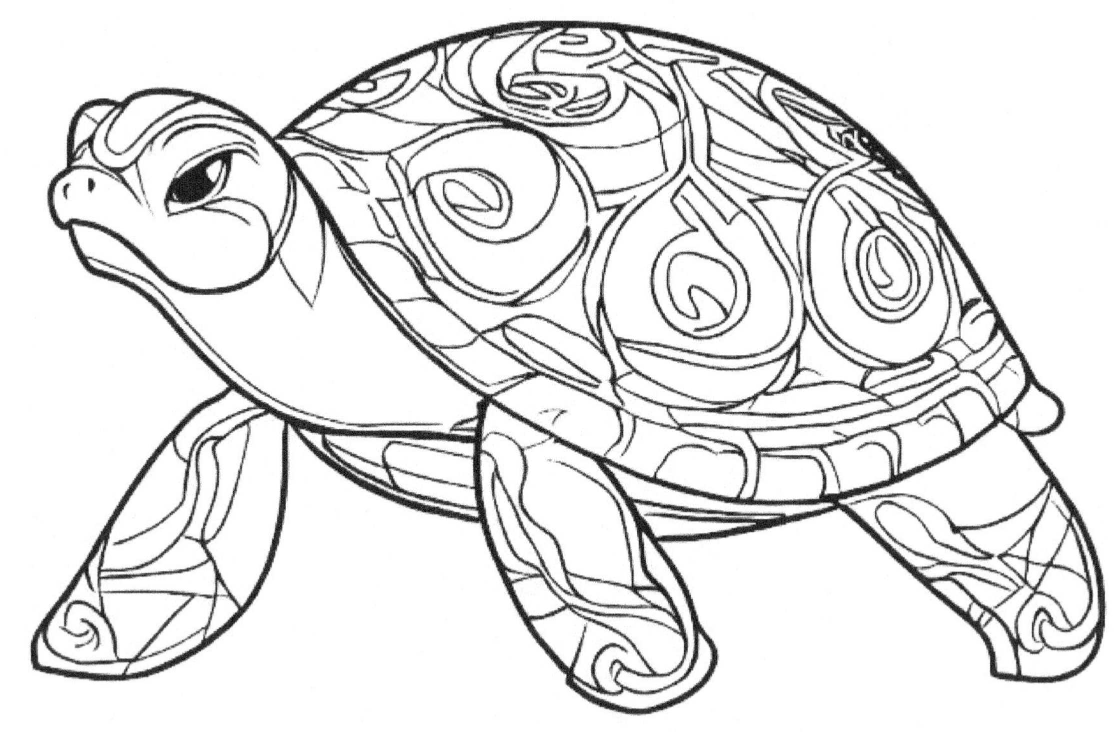

green turtle

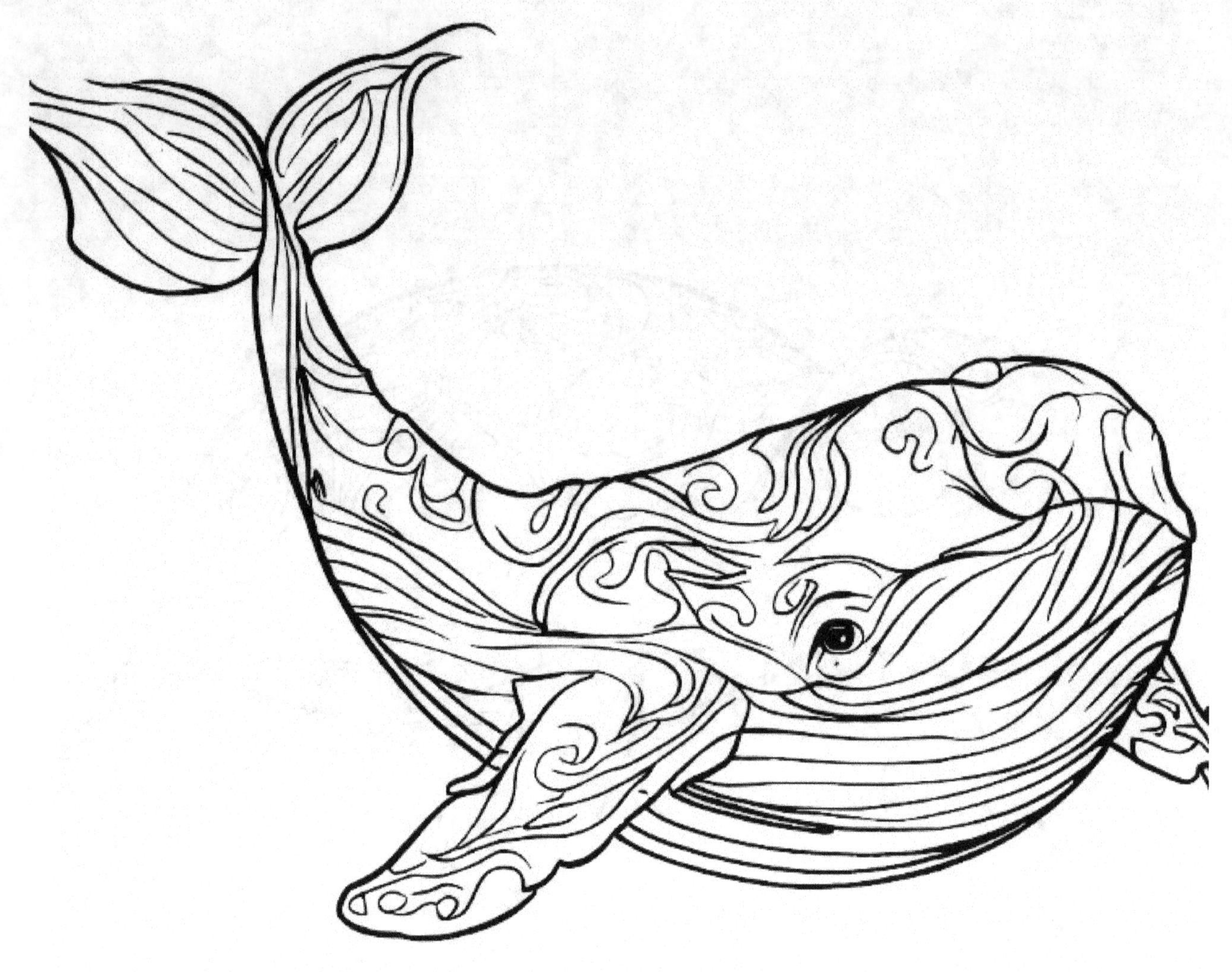

Humpback whale

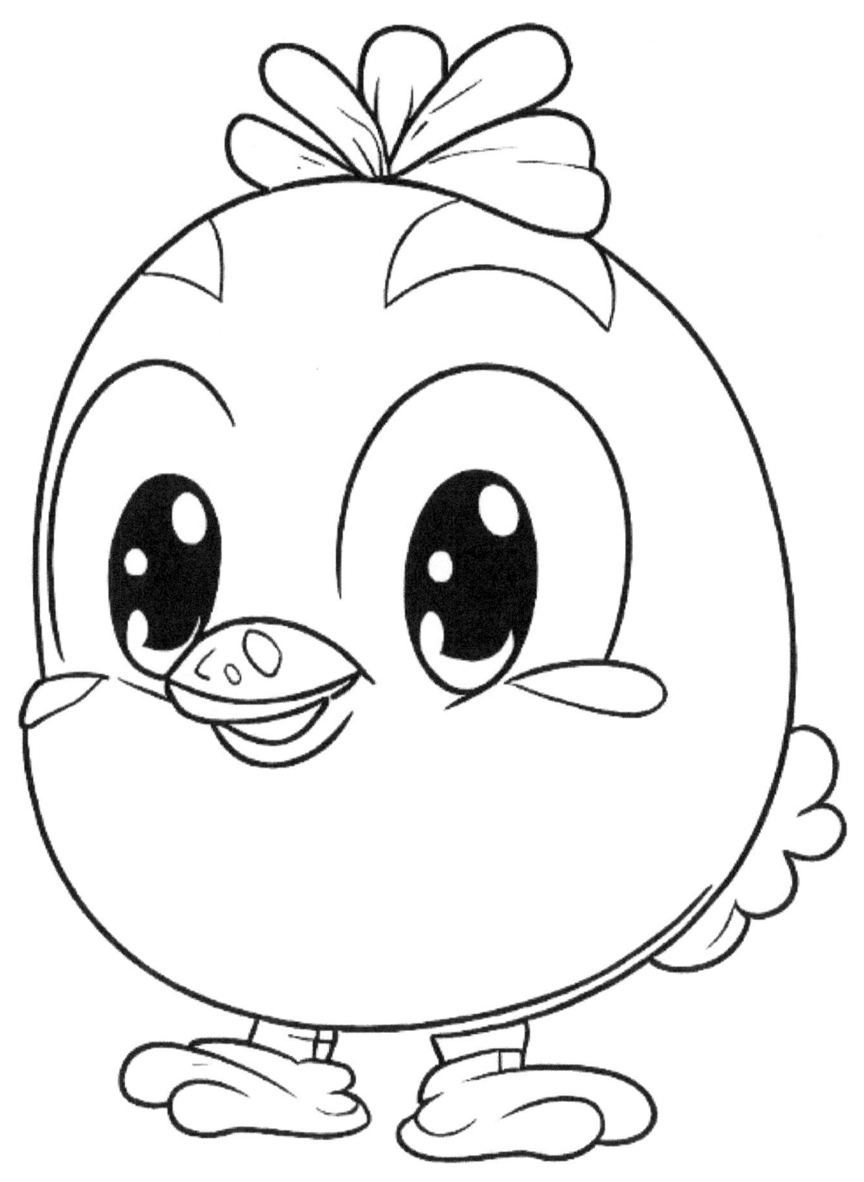

Kiwi

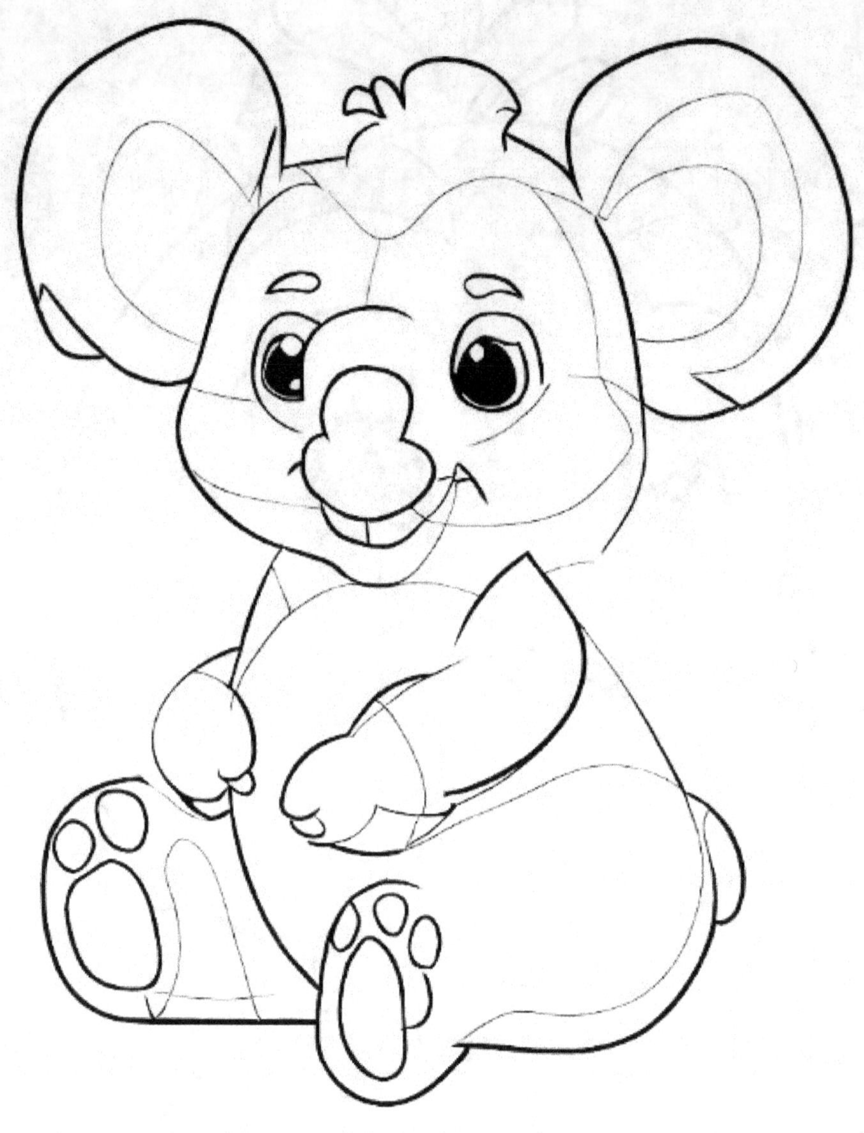

Koala

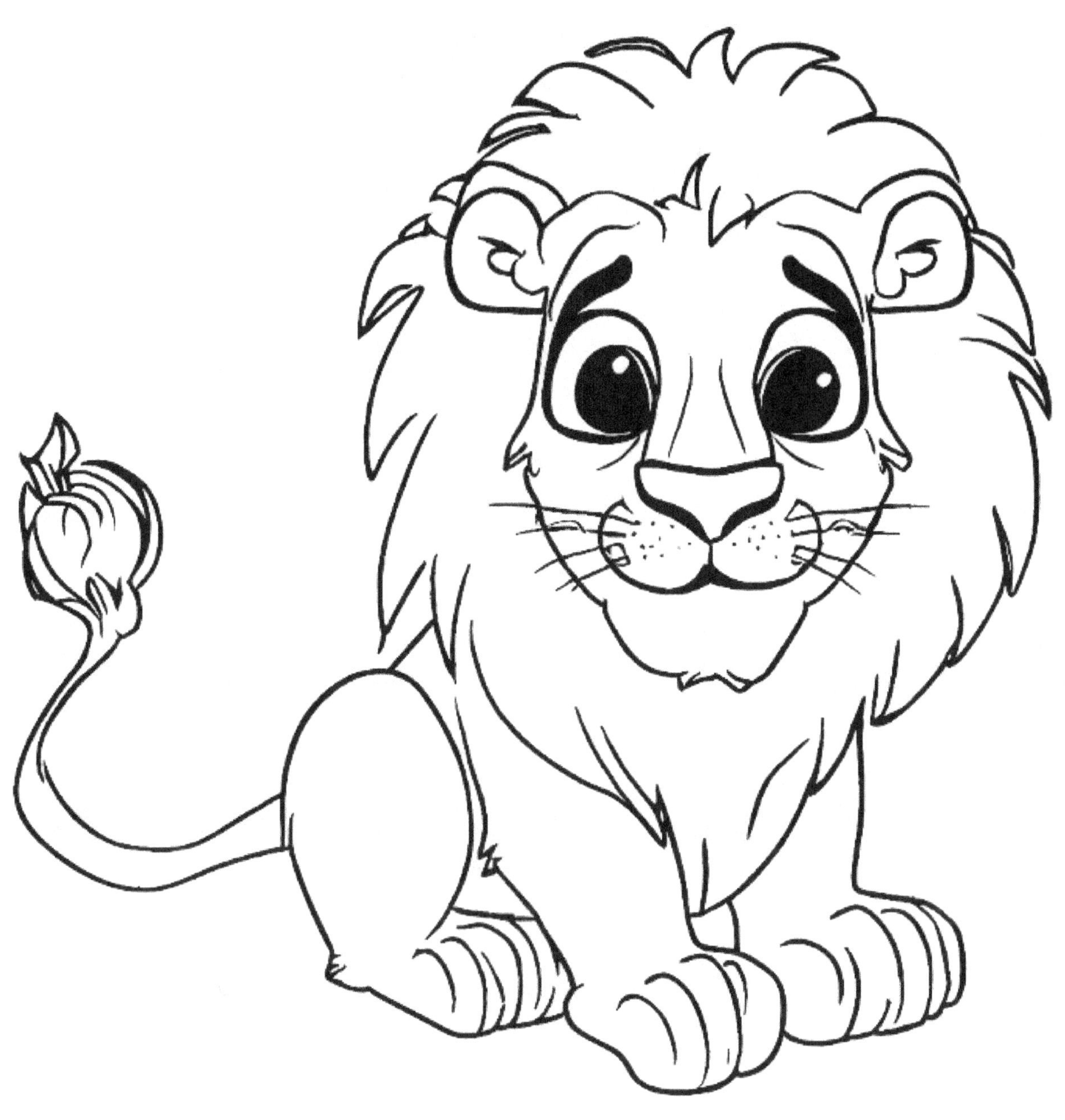

lion

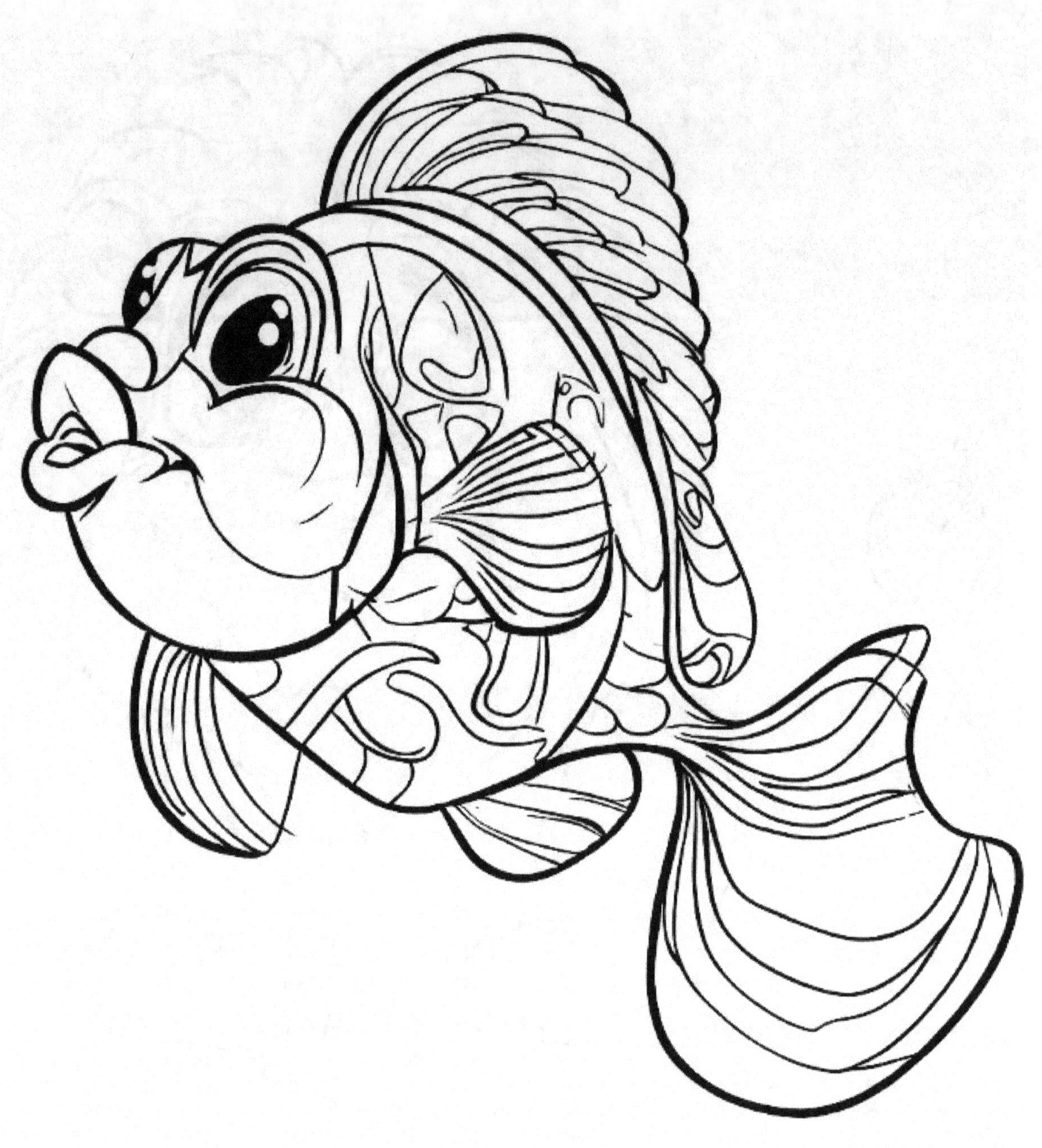

Mandarin
fish

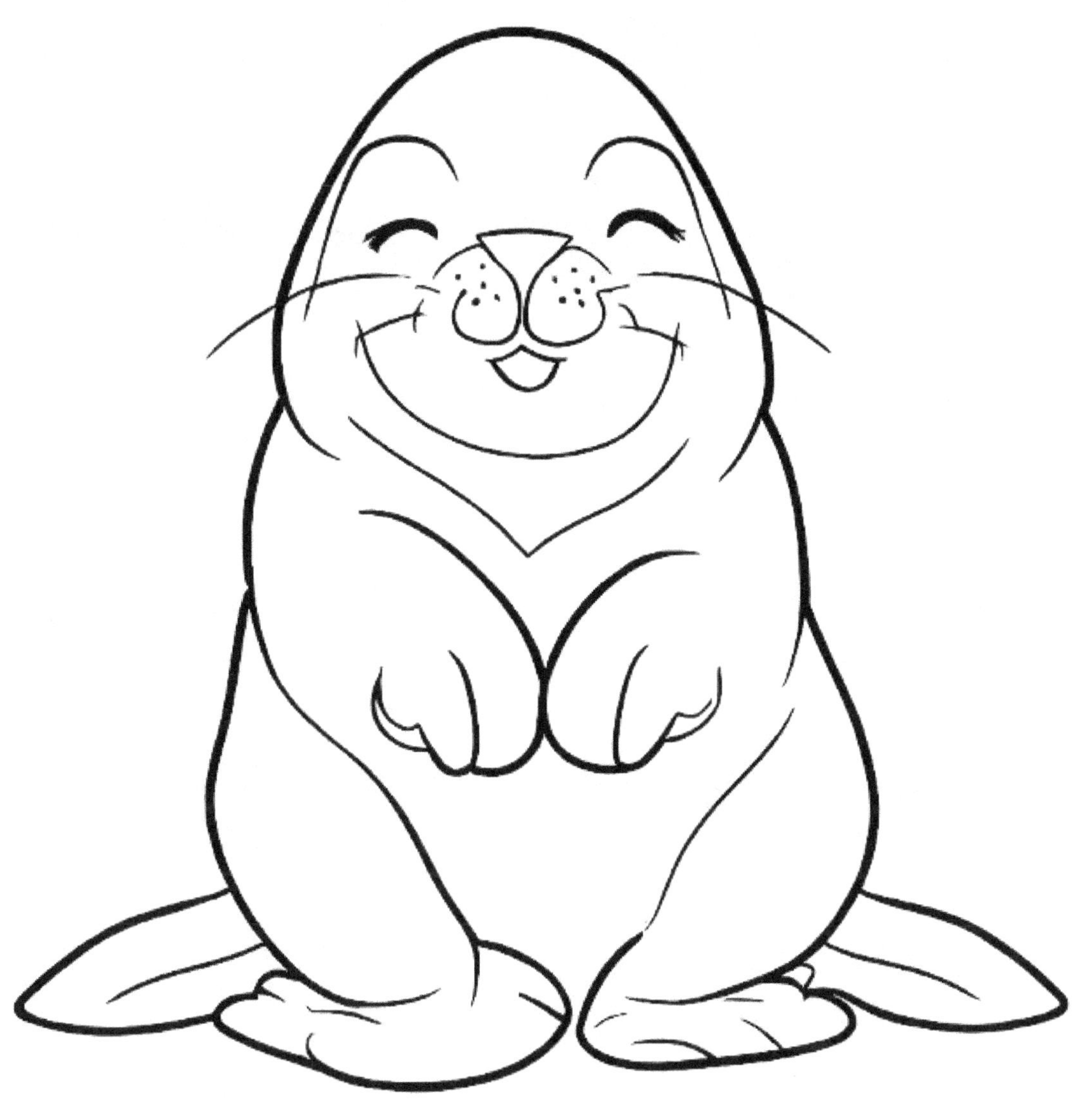

mediterranean
monk seal

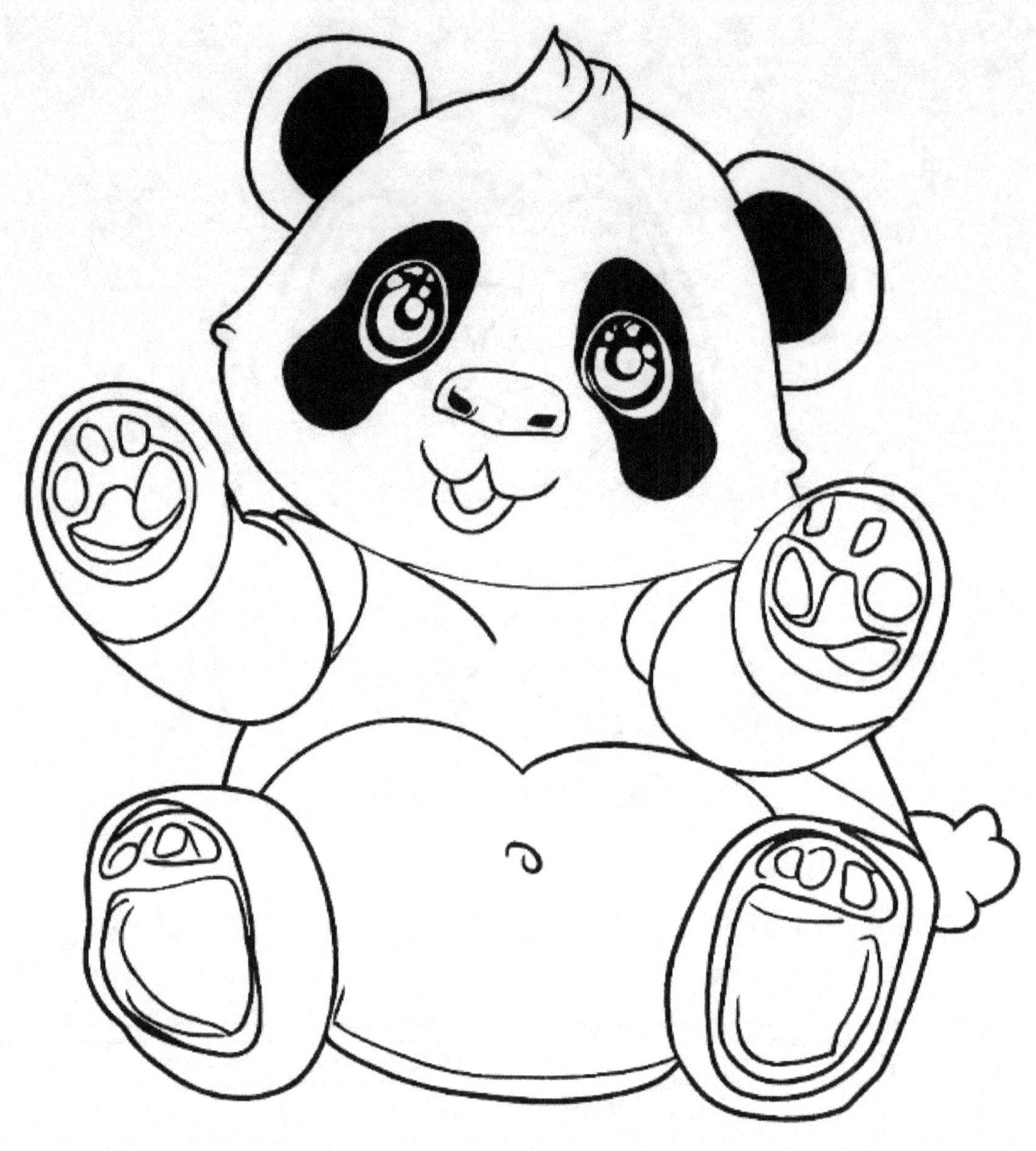

panda

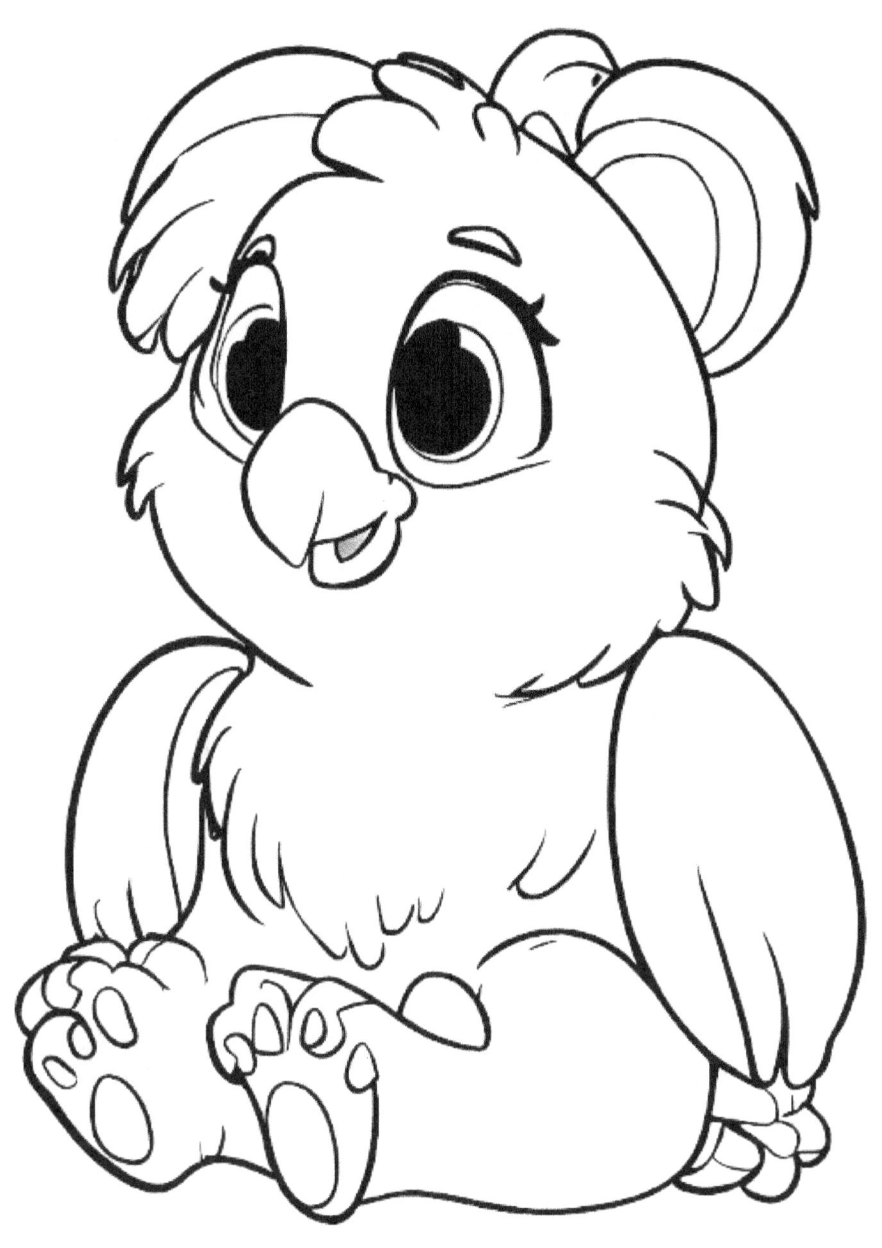

parrot

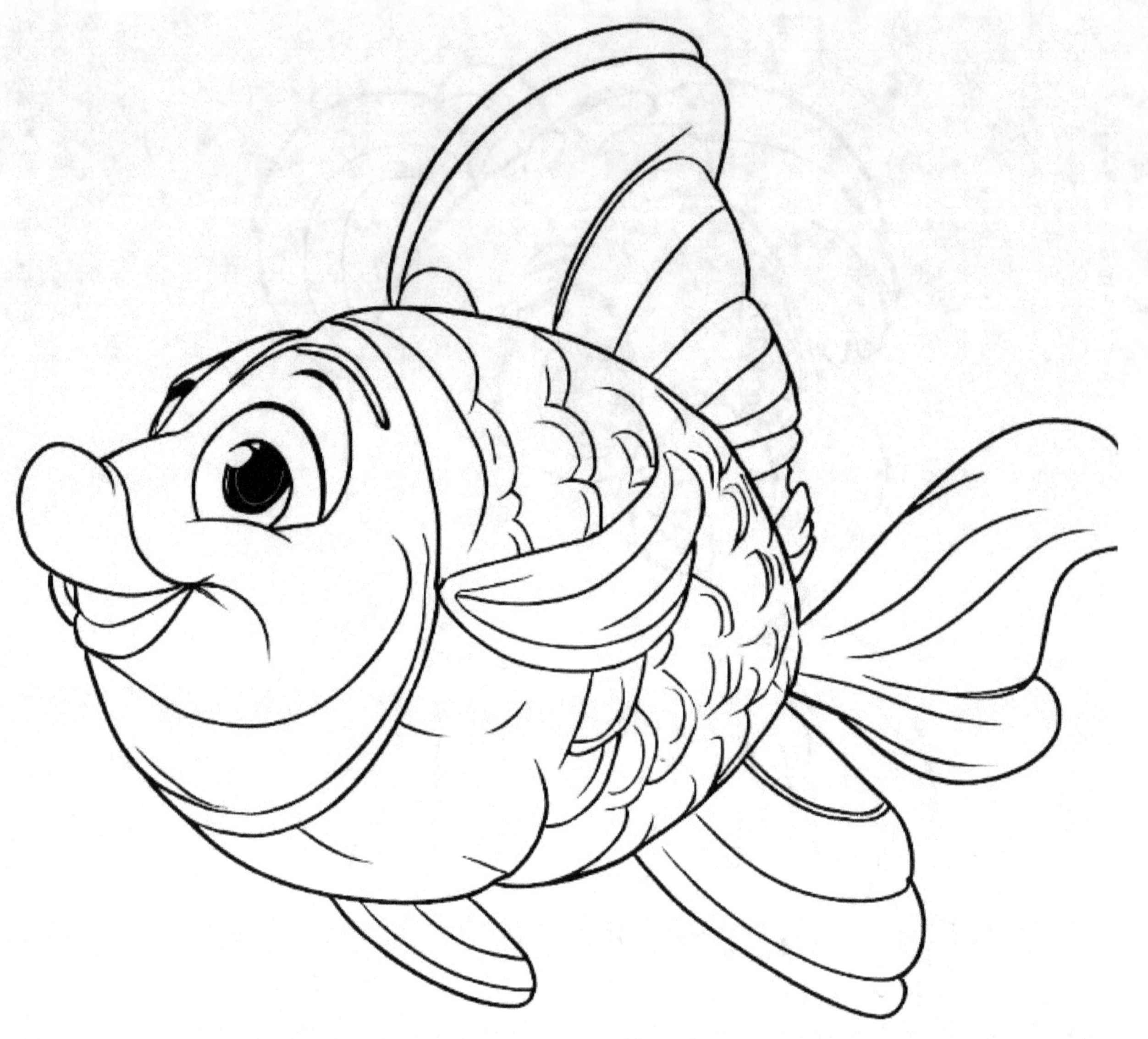

Parrotfish

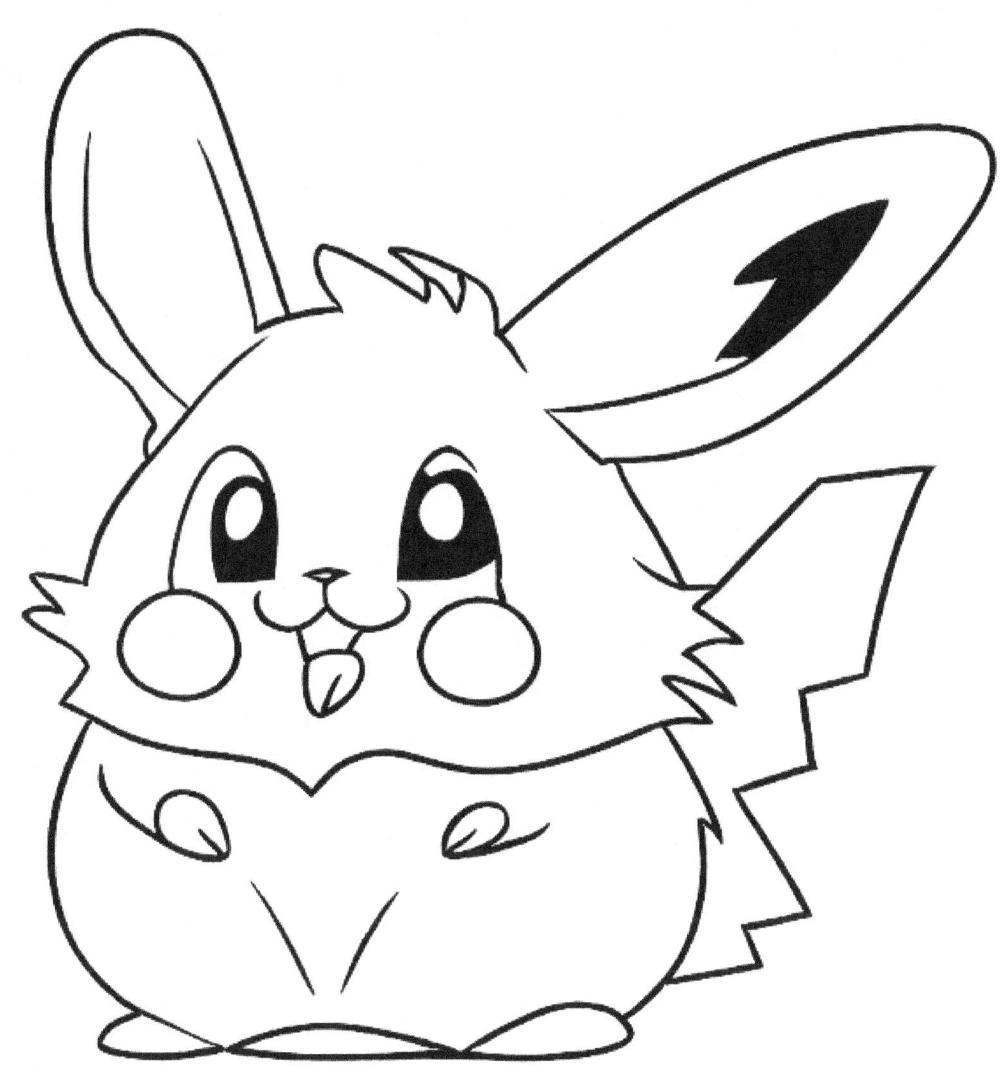

Pika

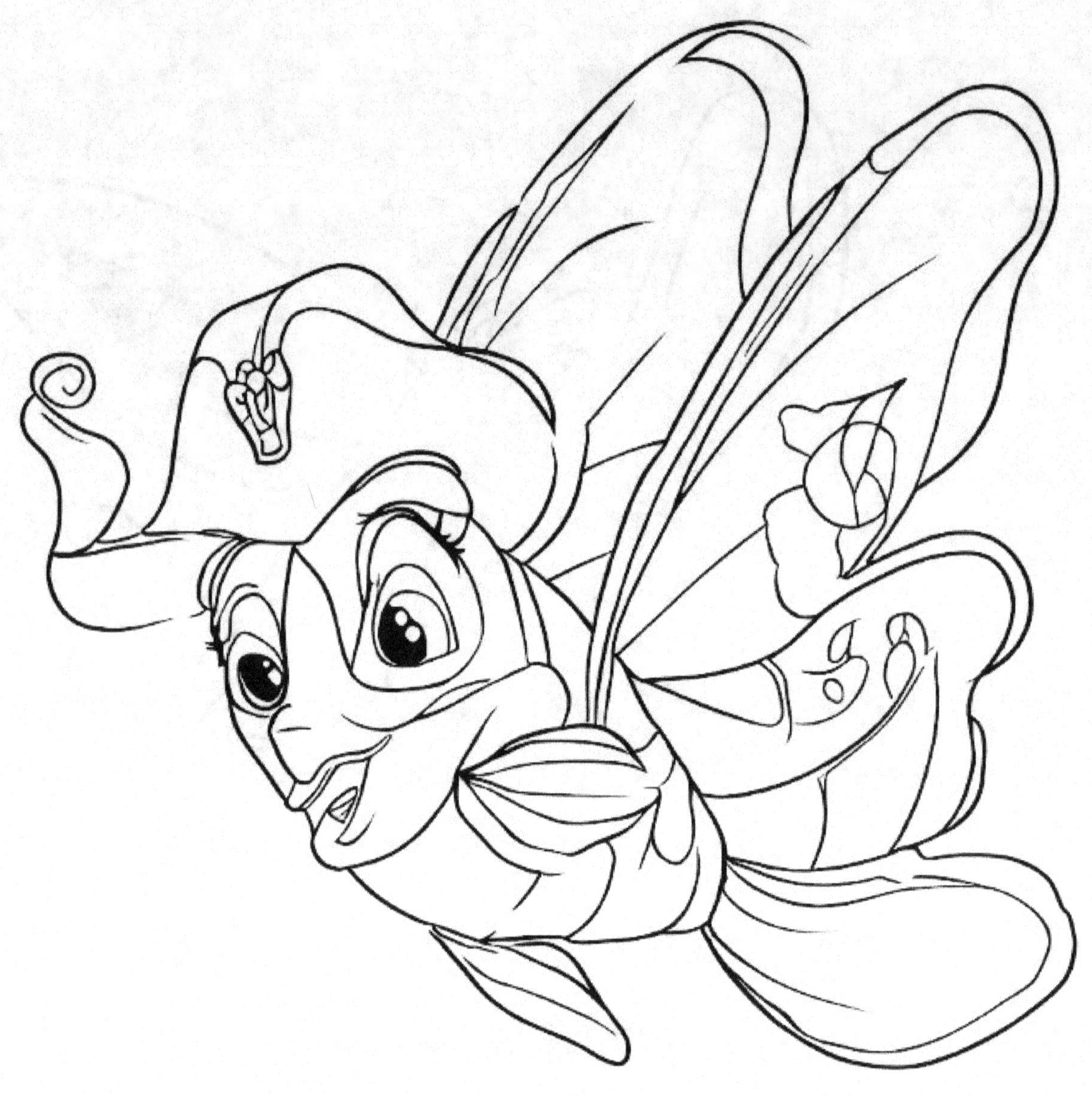

Pirate
butterflyfish

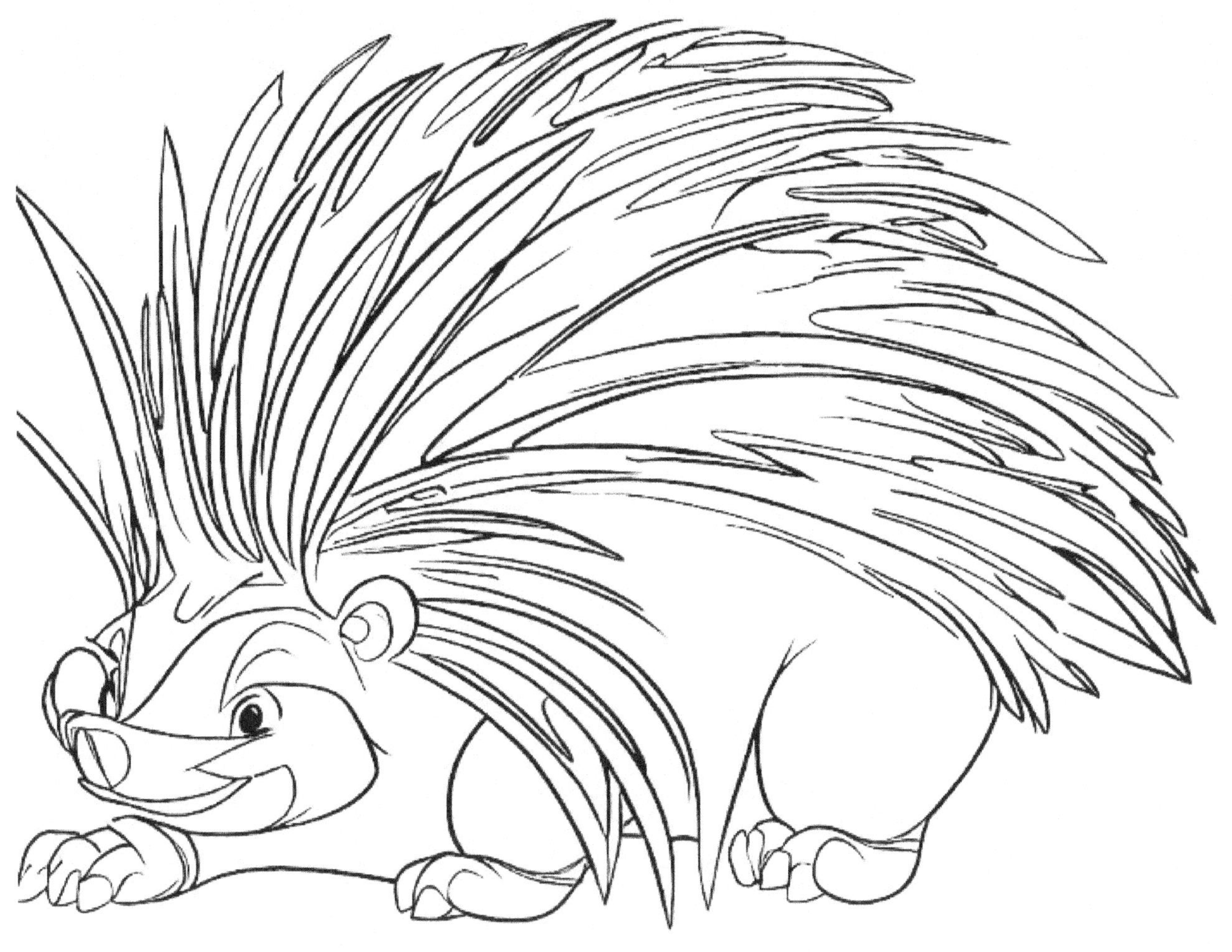

Porcupine

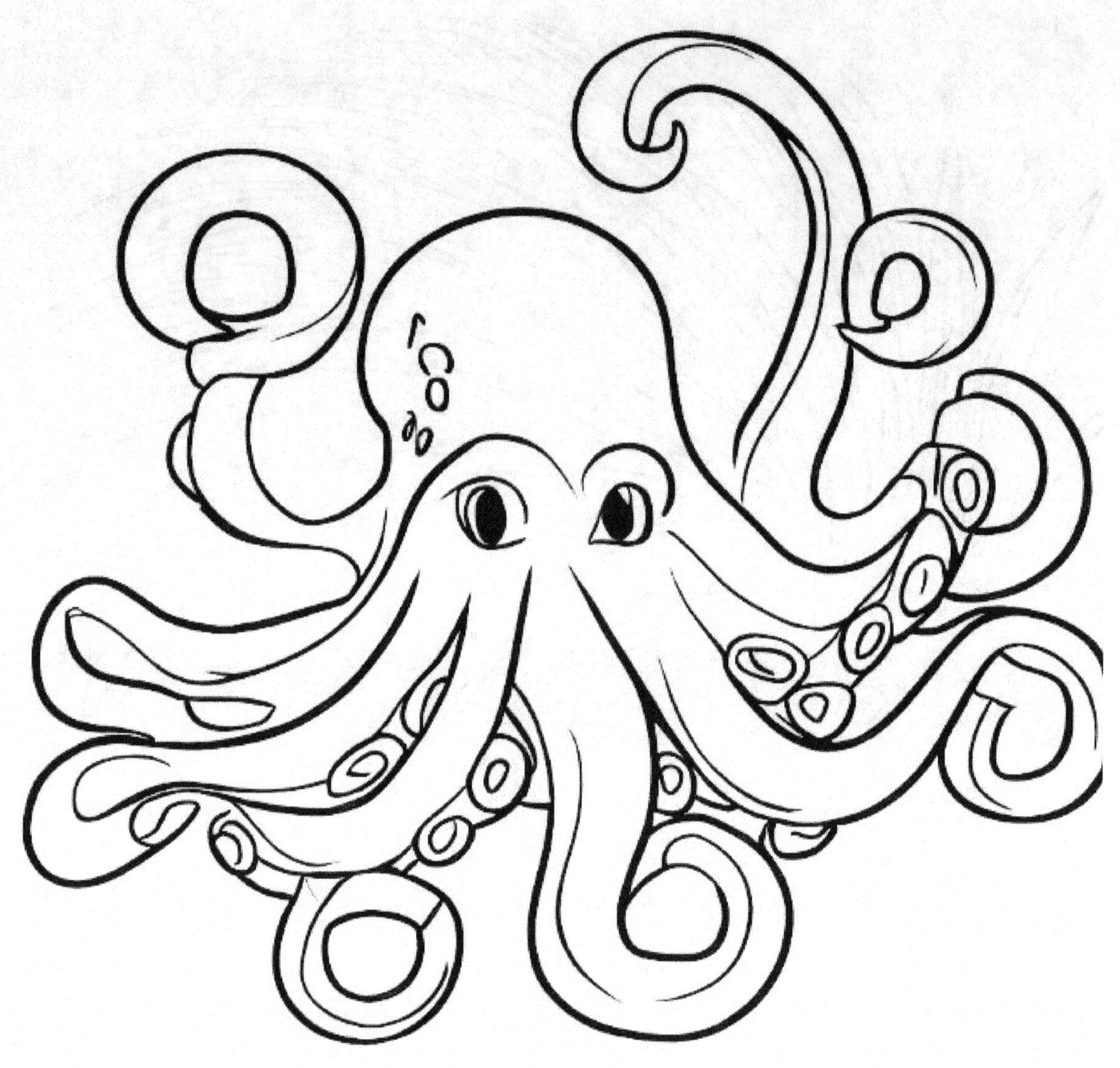

Powder

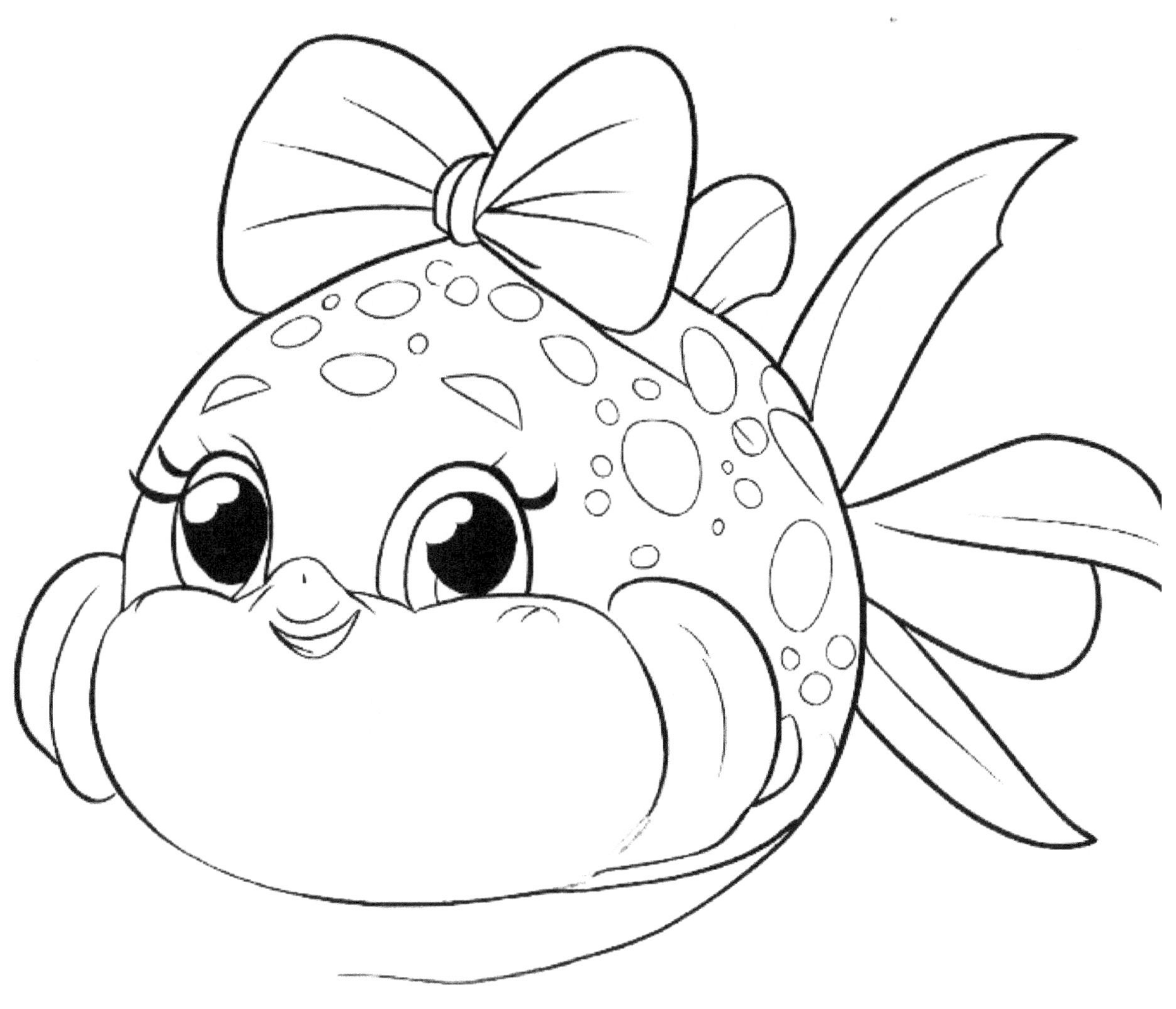

Puffer fish

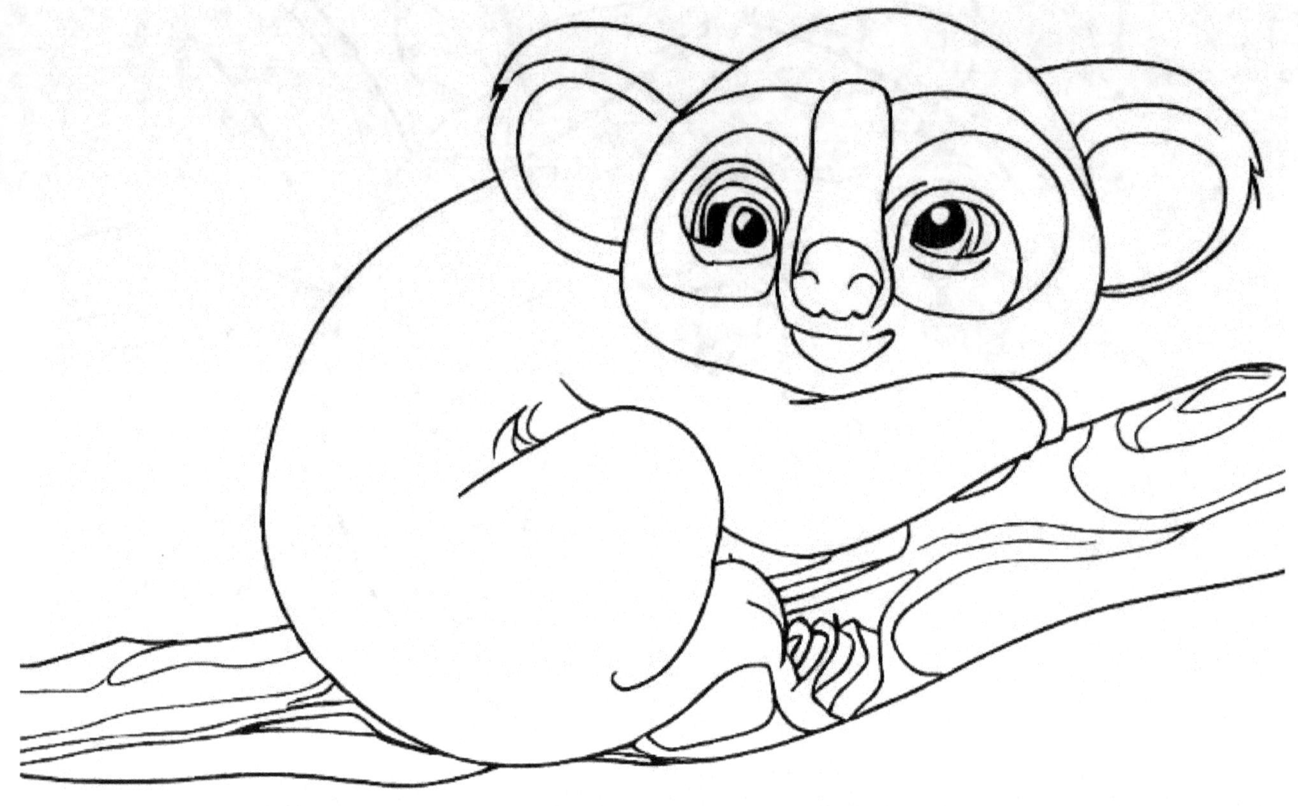

Pygmy slow loris

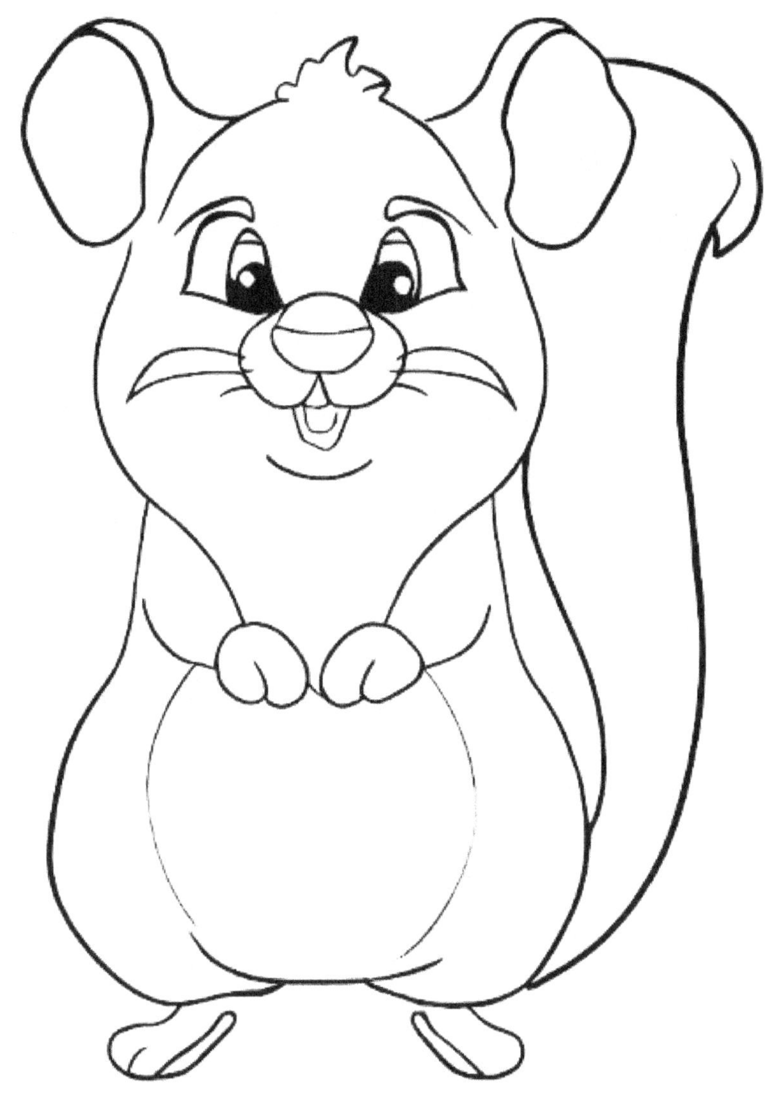

Quokka

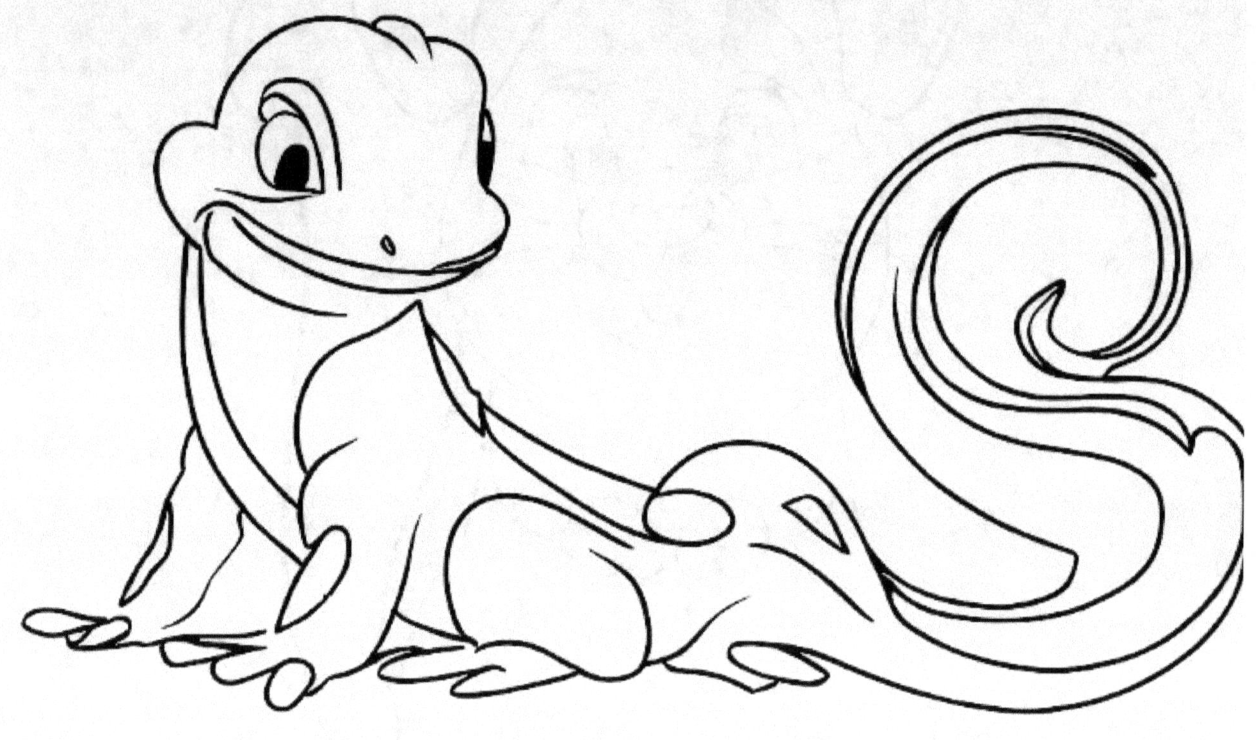

salamander

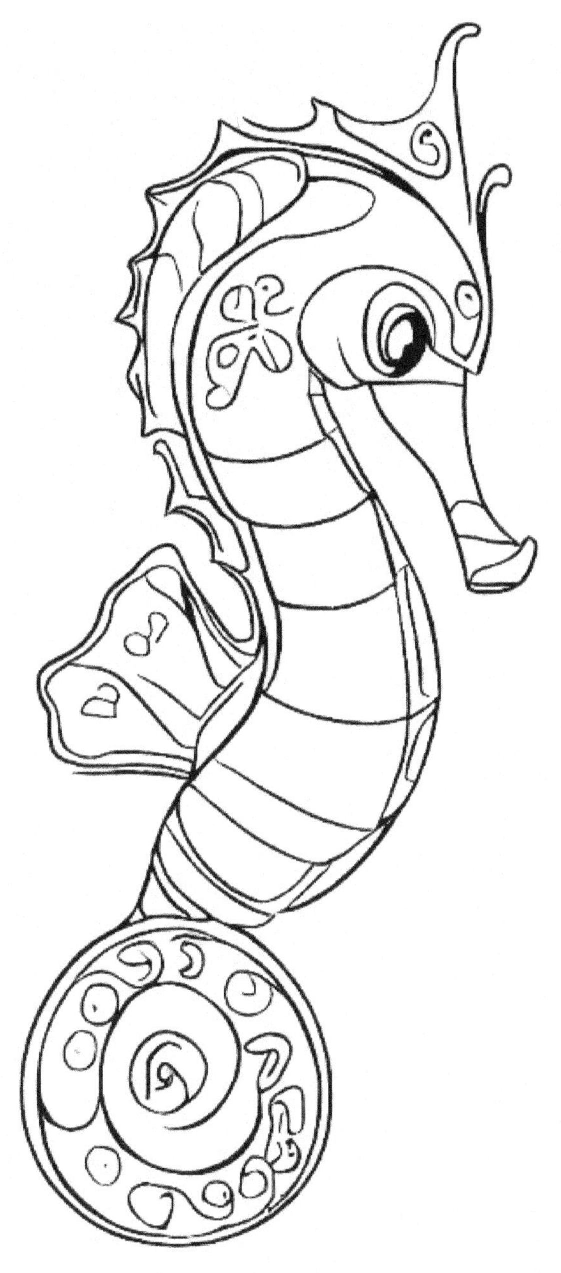

seahorse

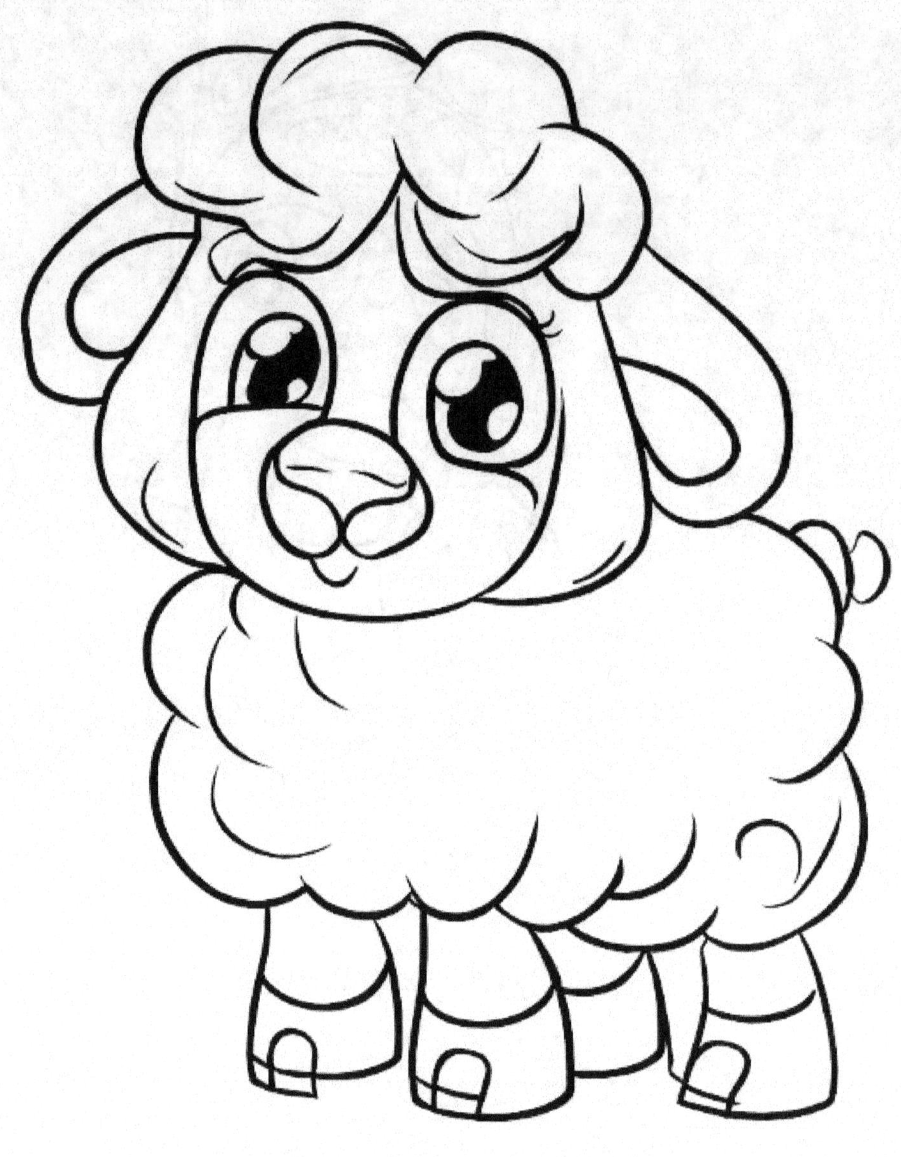

sheep

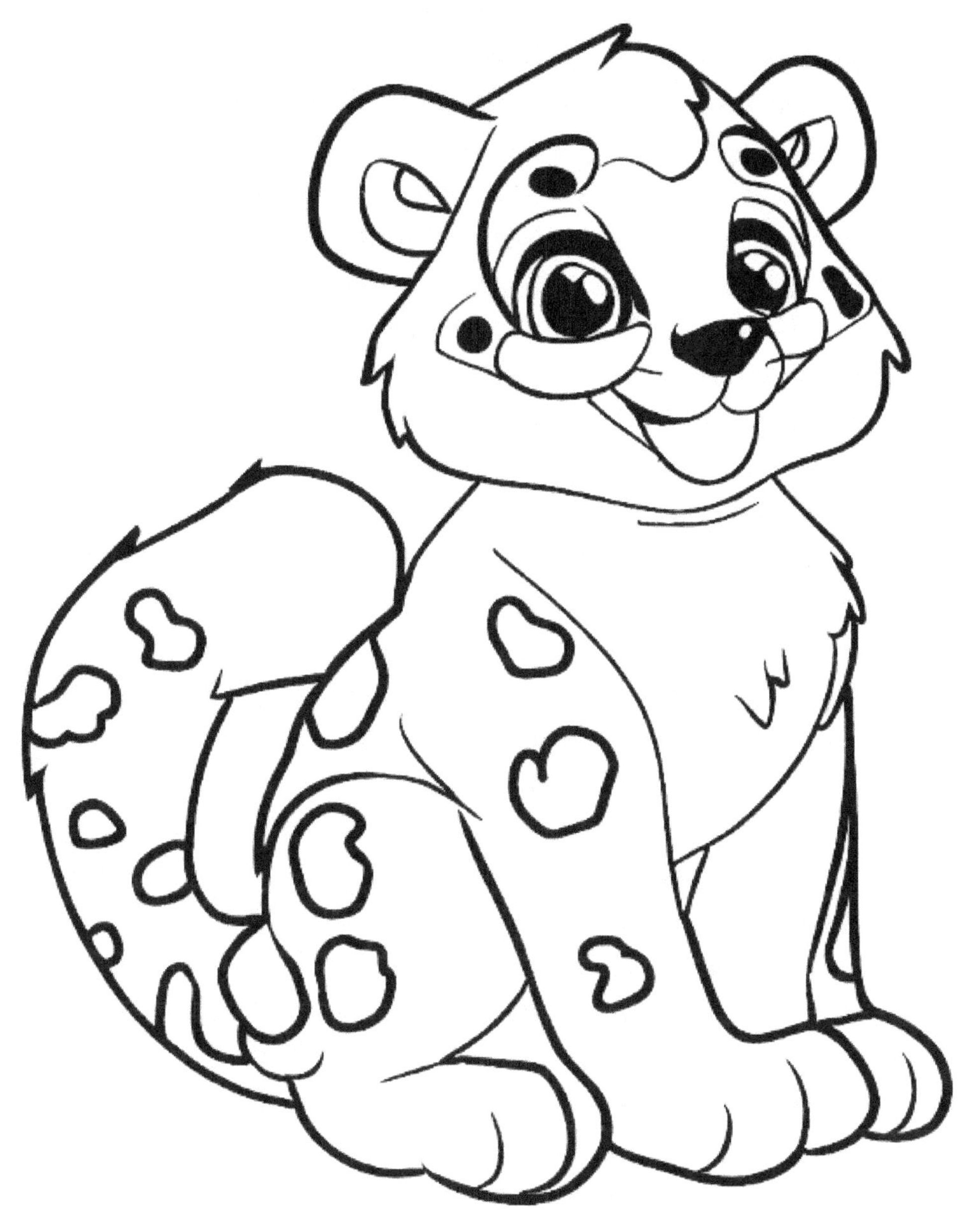

snow leopard

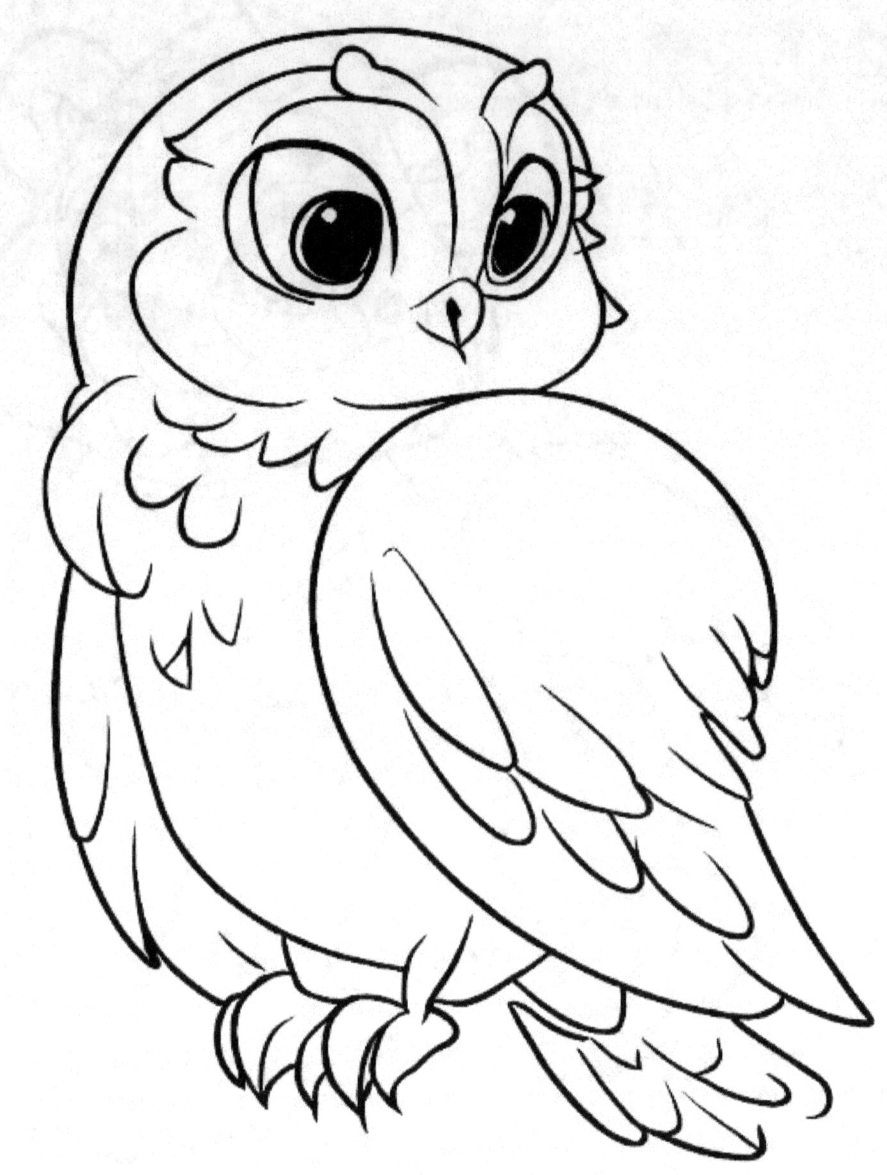

snow owl

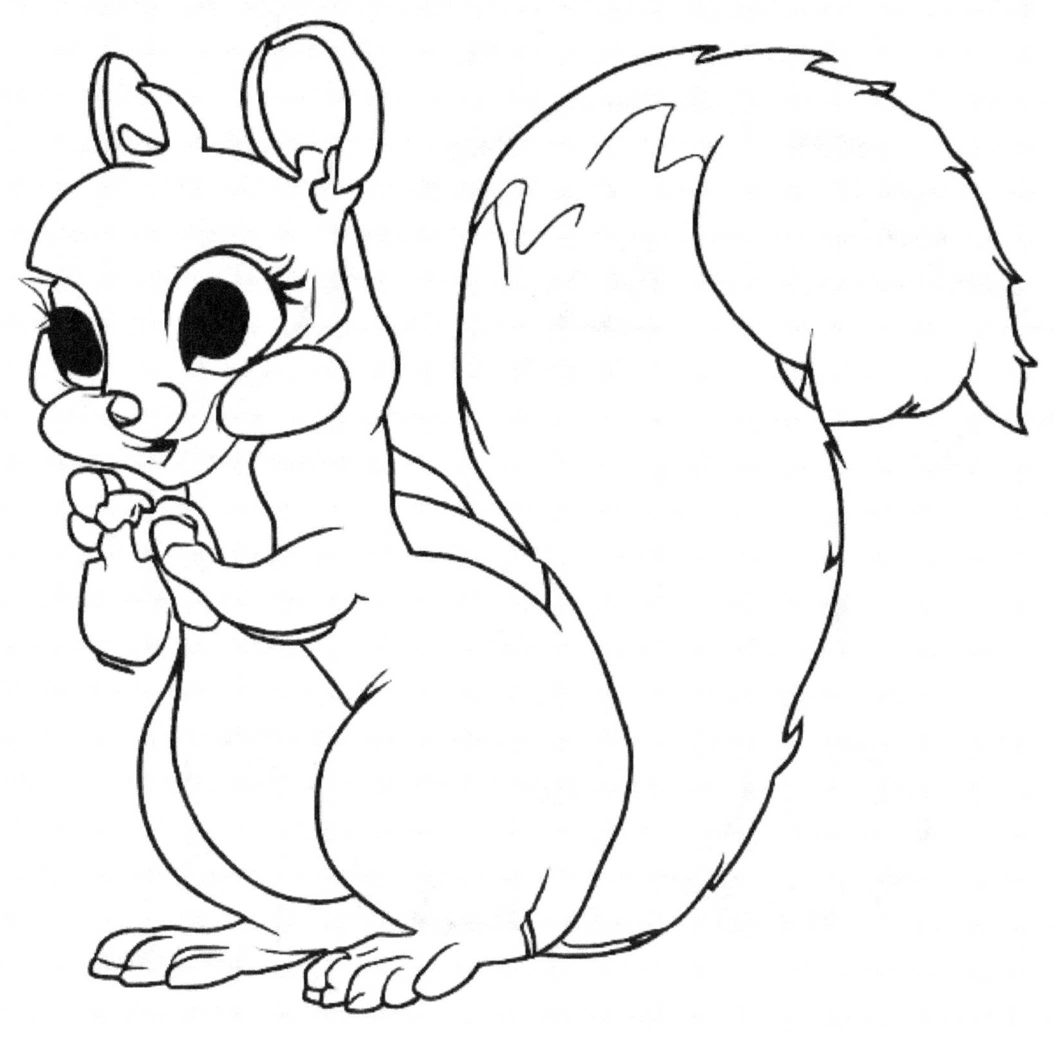

Squirrel

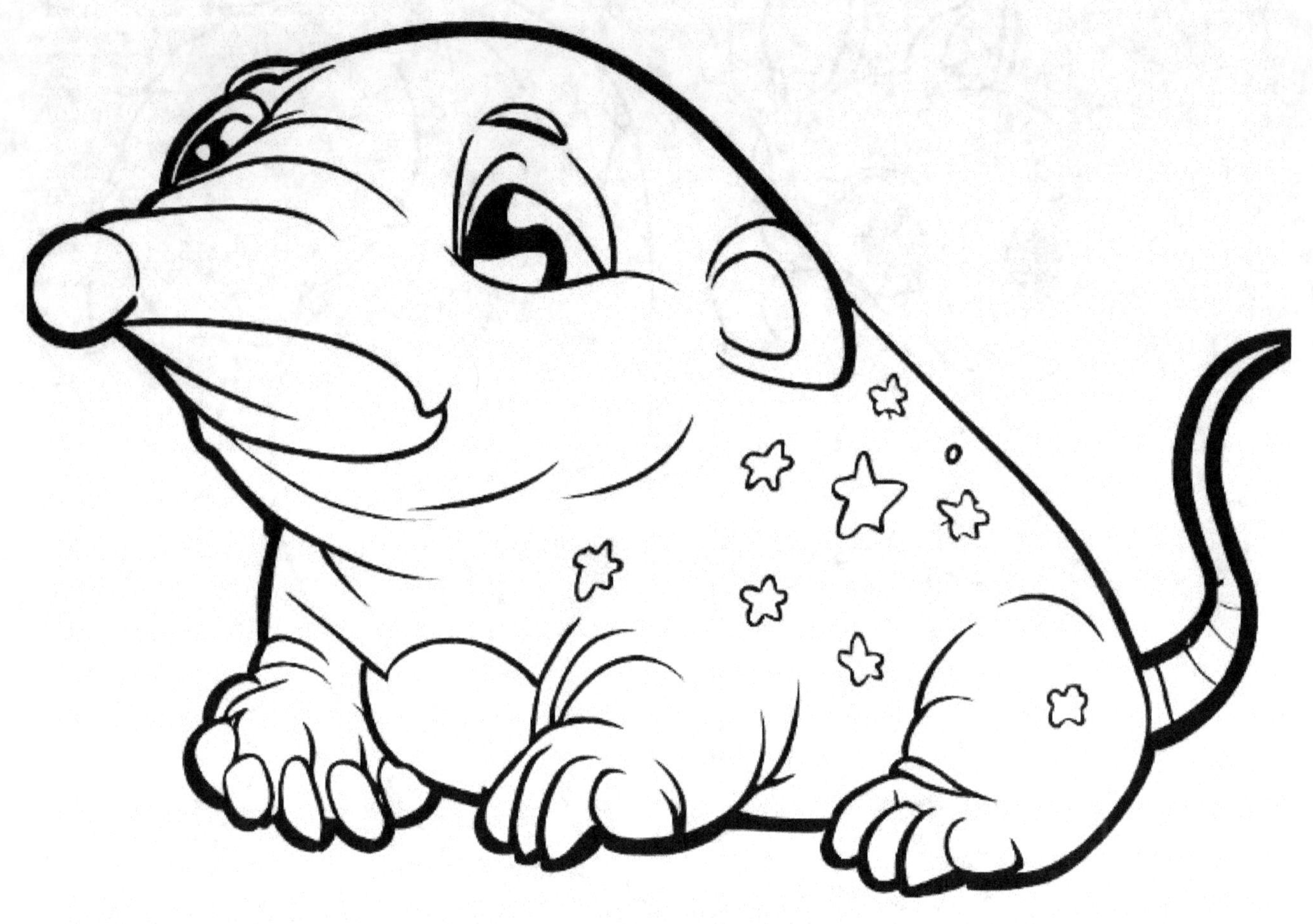

star nosed
mole

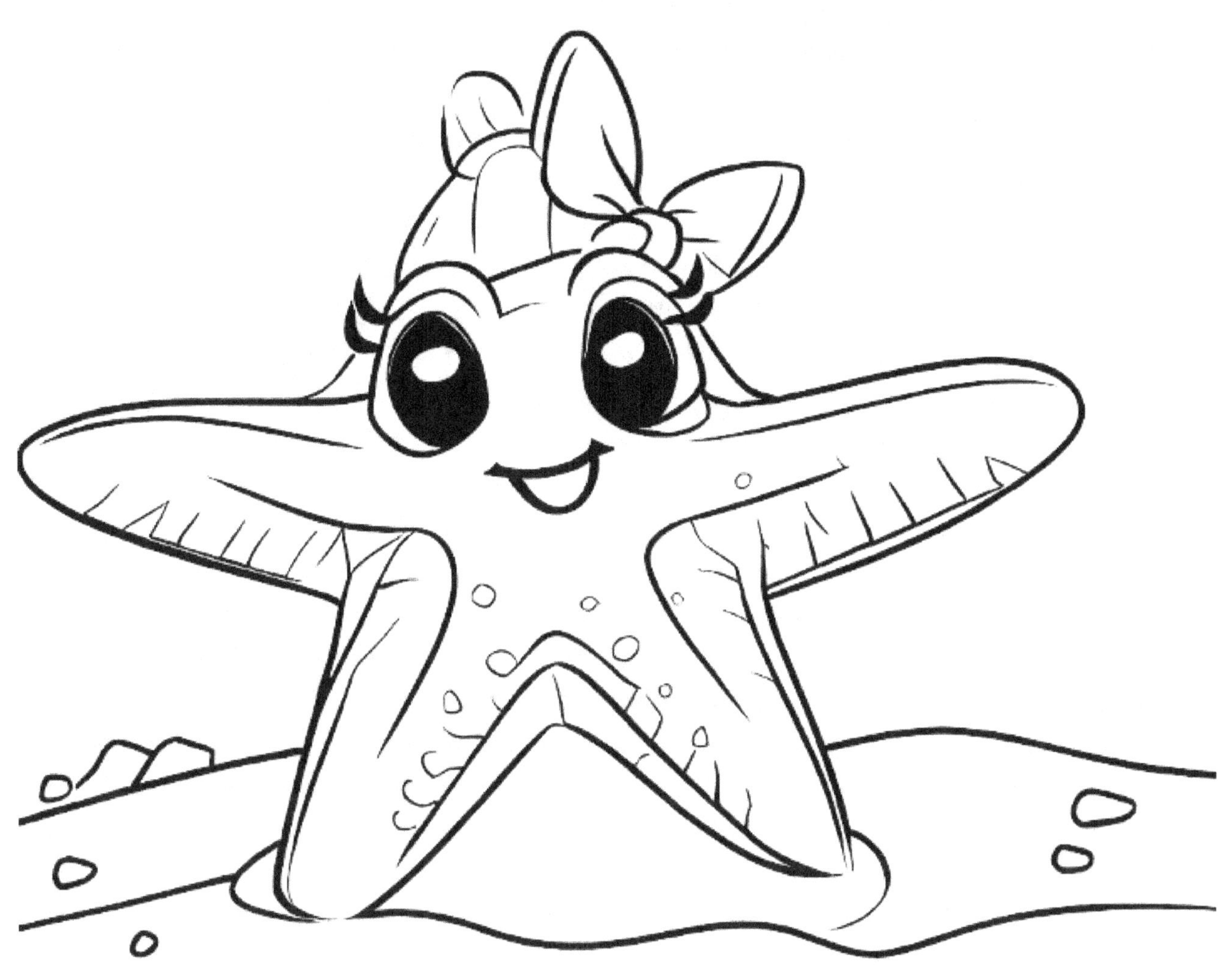

Starfish

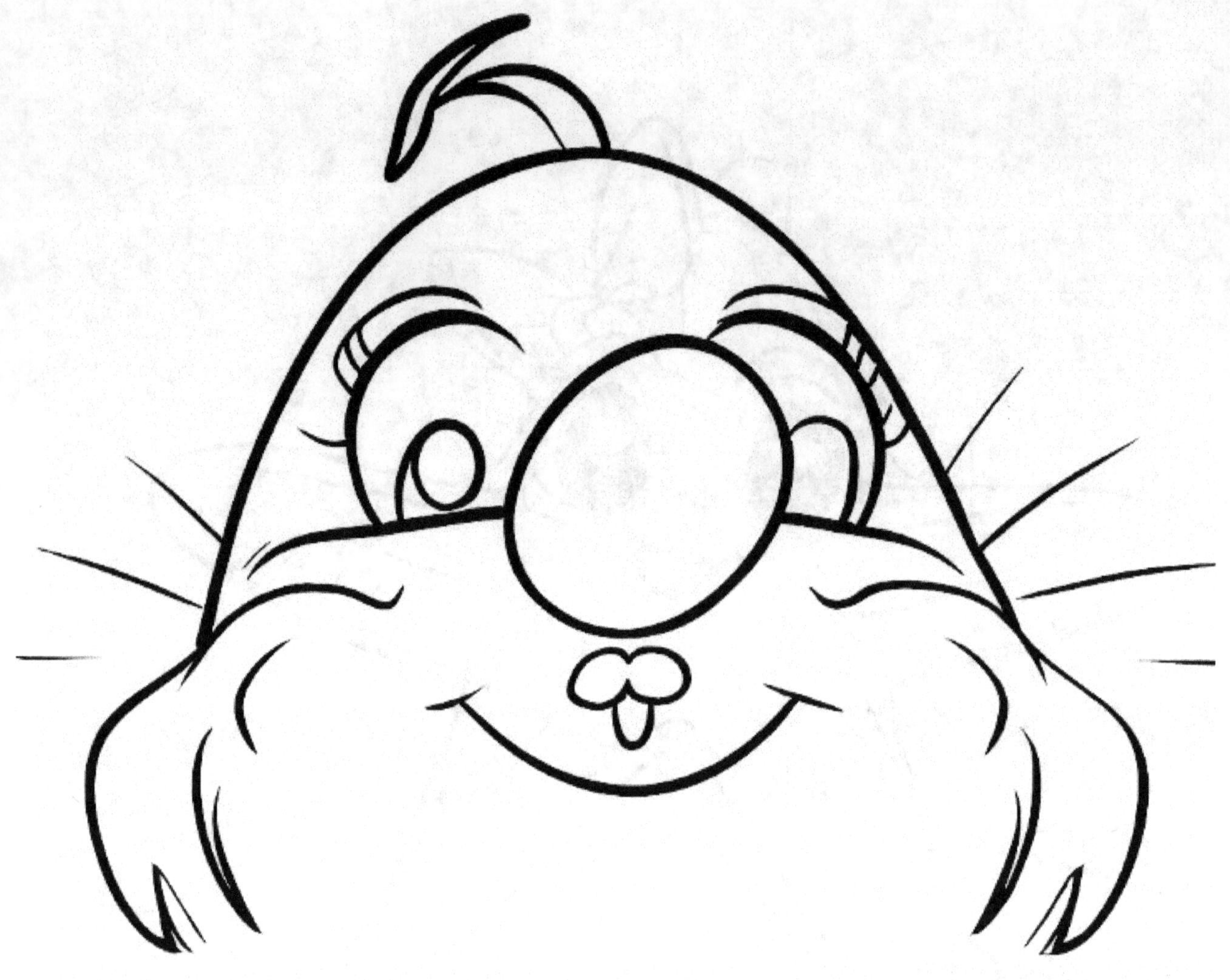

star-nosed mole

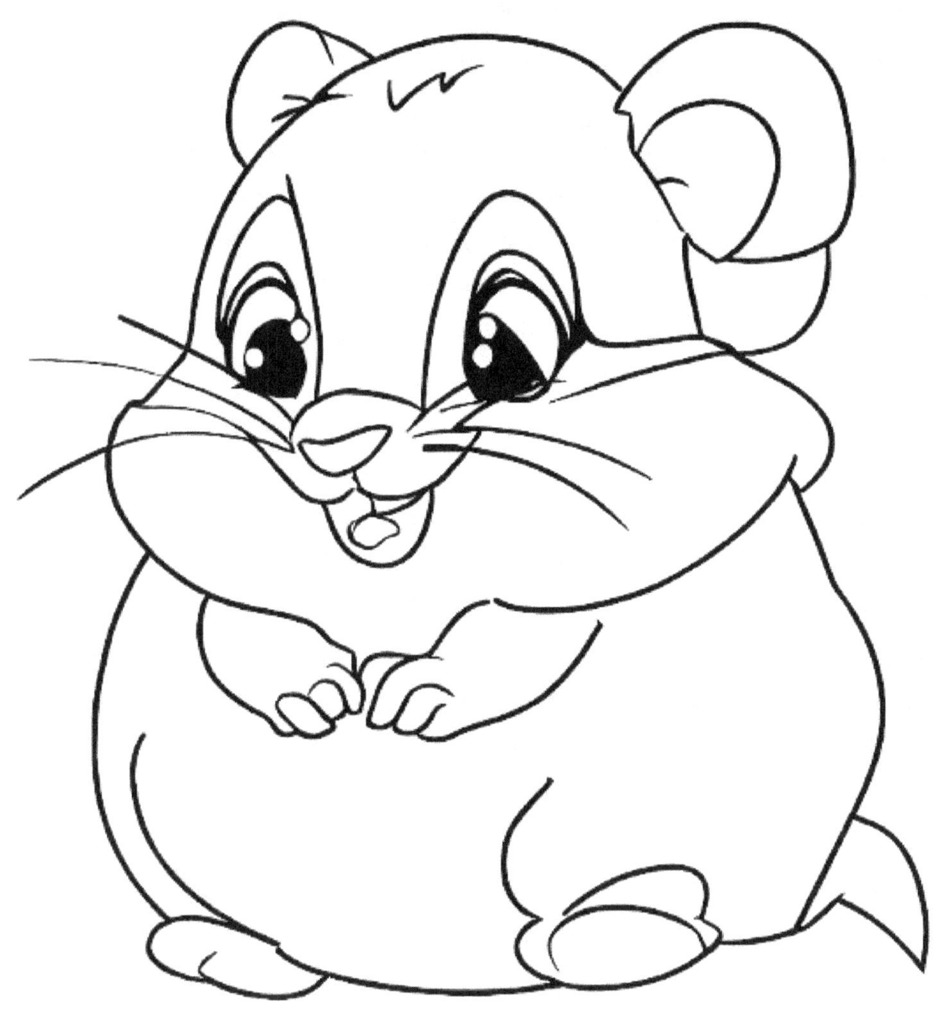

syrian
hamster

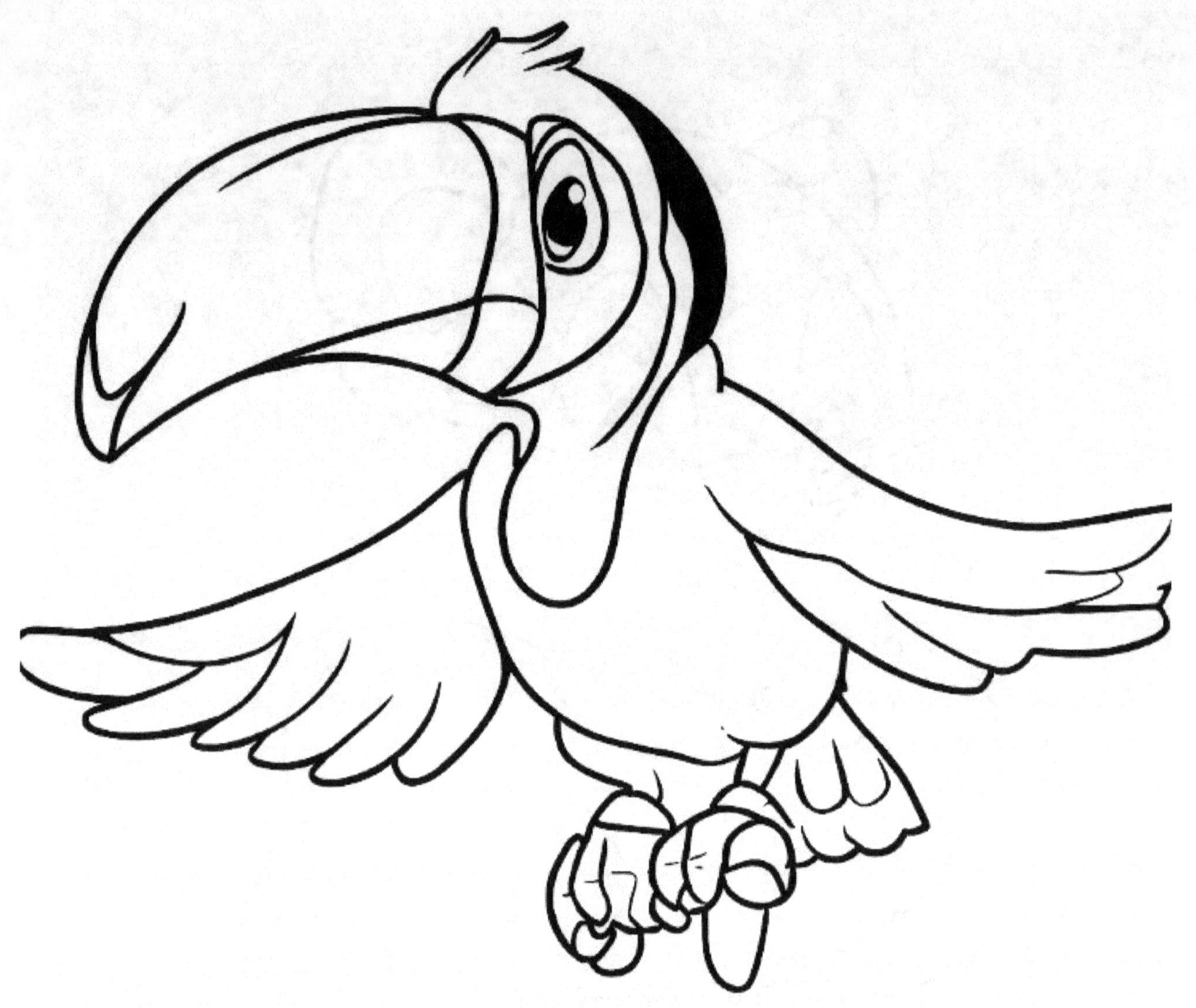

Toucan

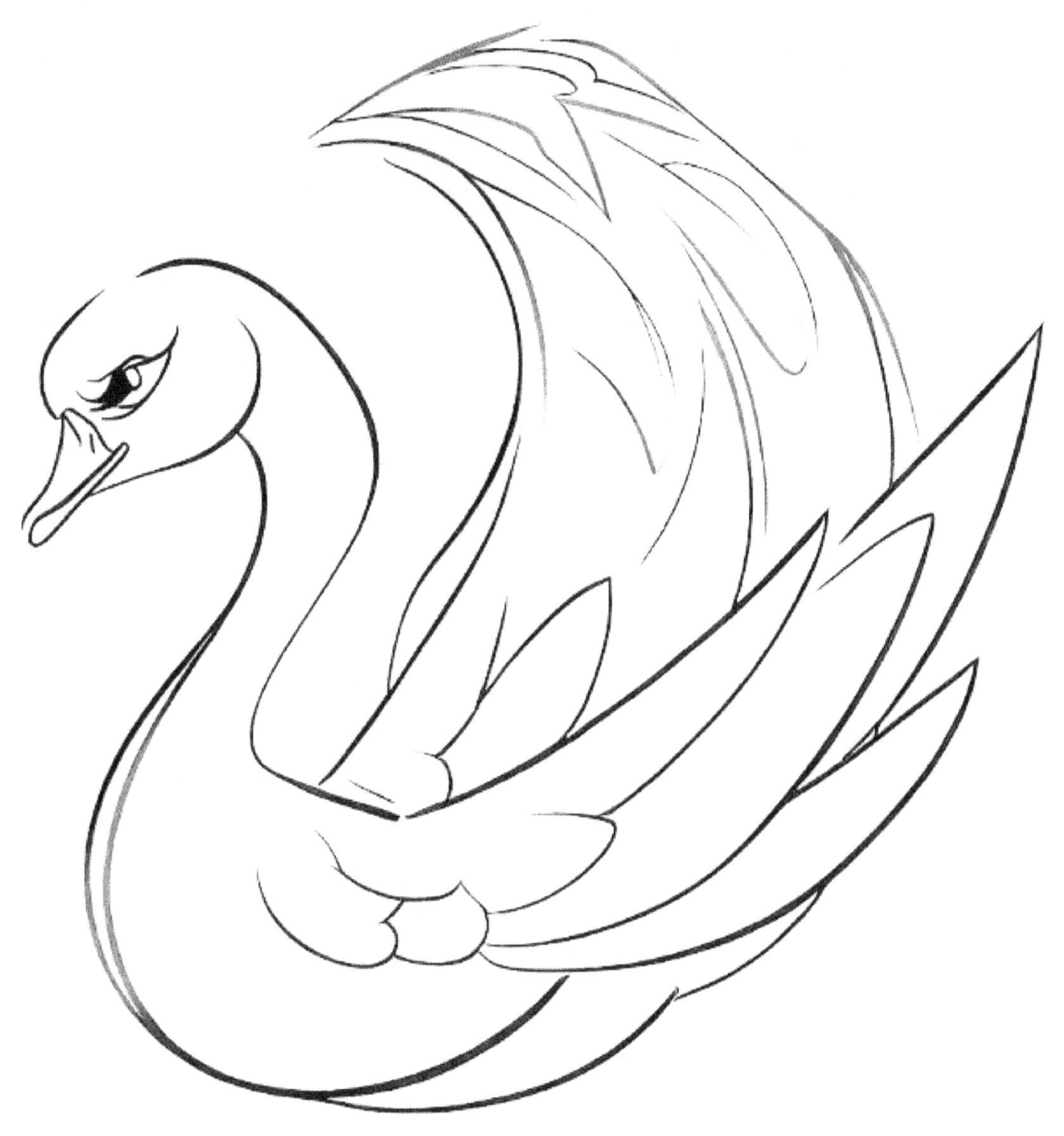

white swan

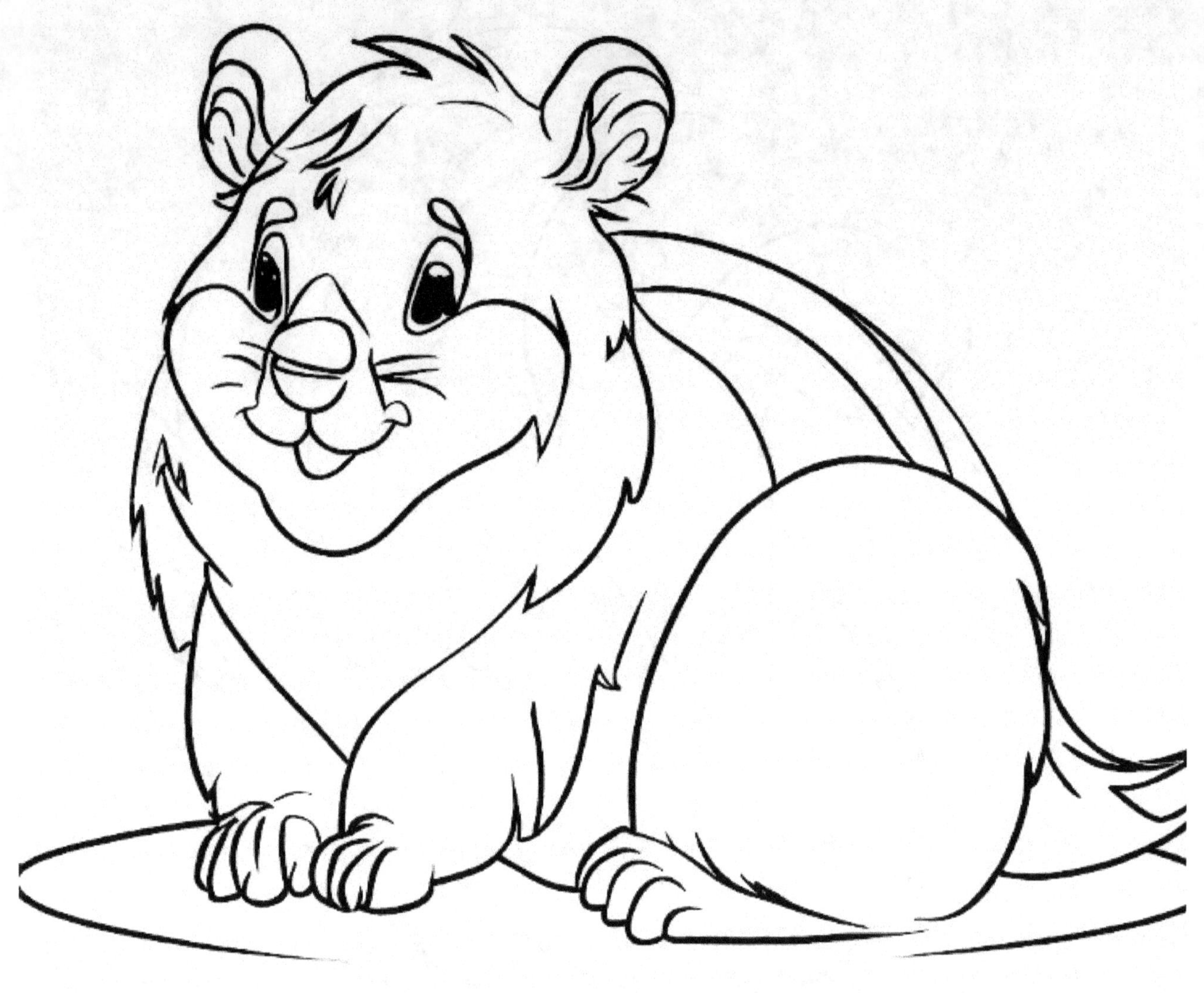

wombat

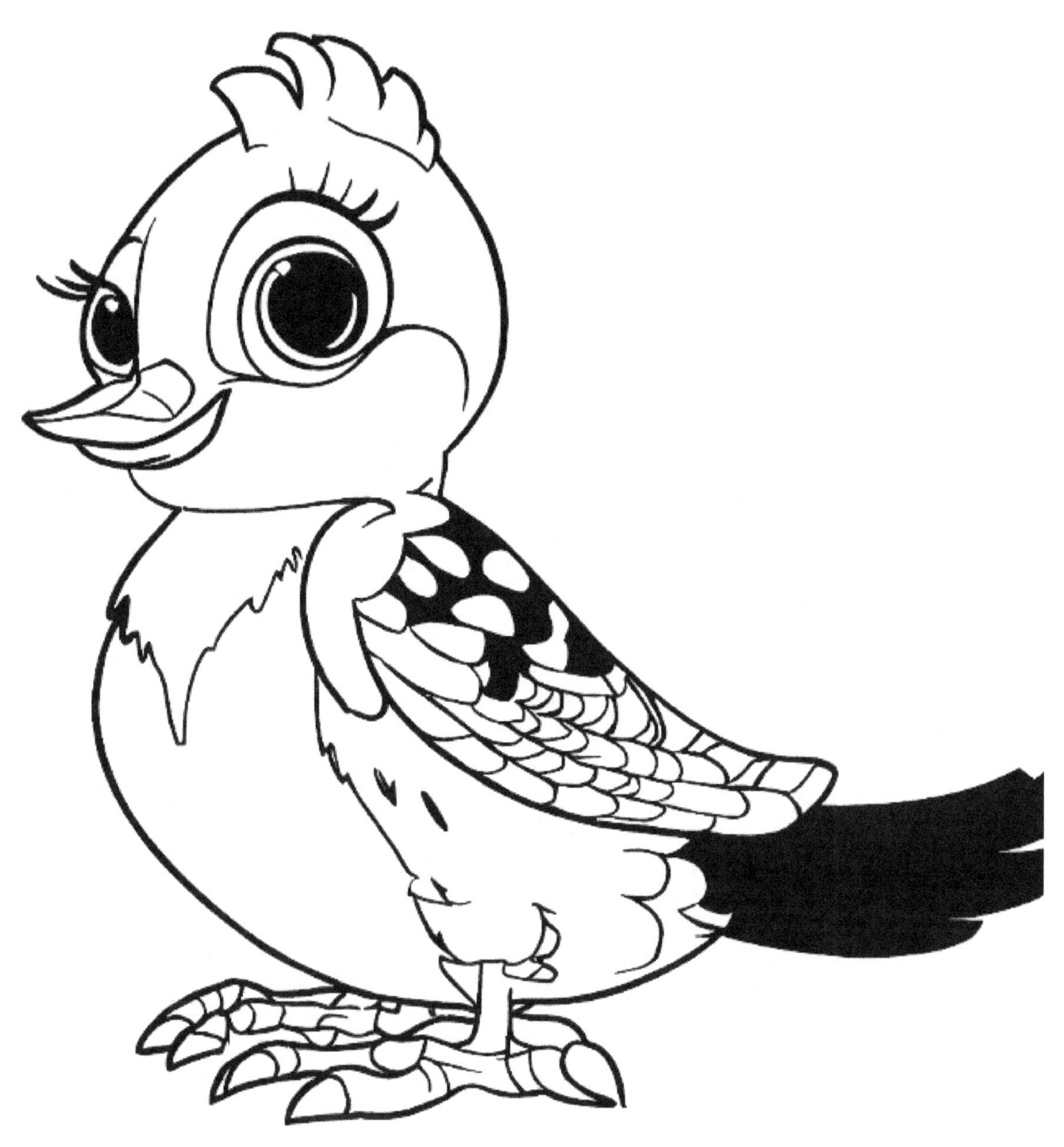

woodpecker

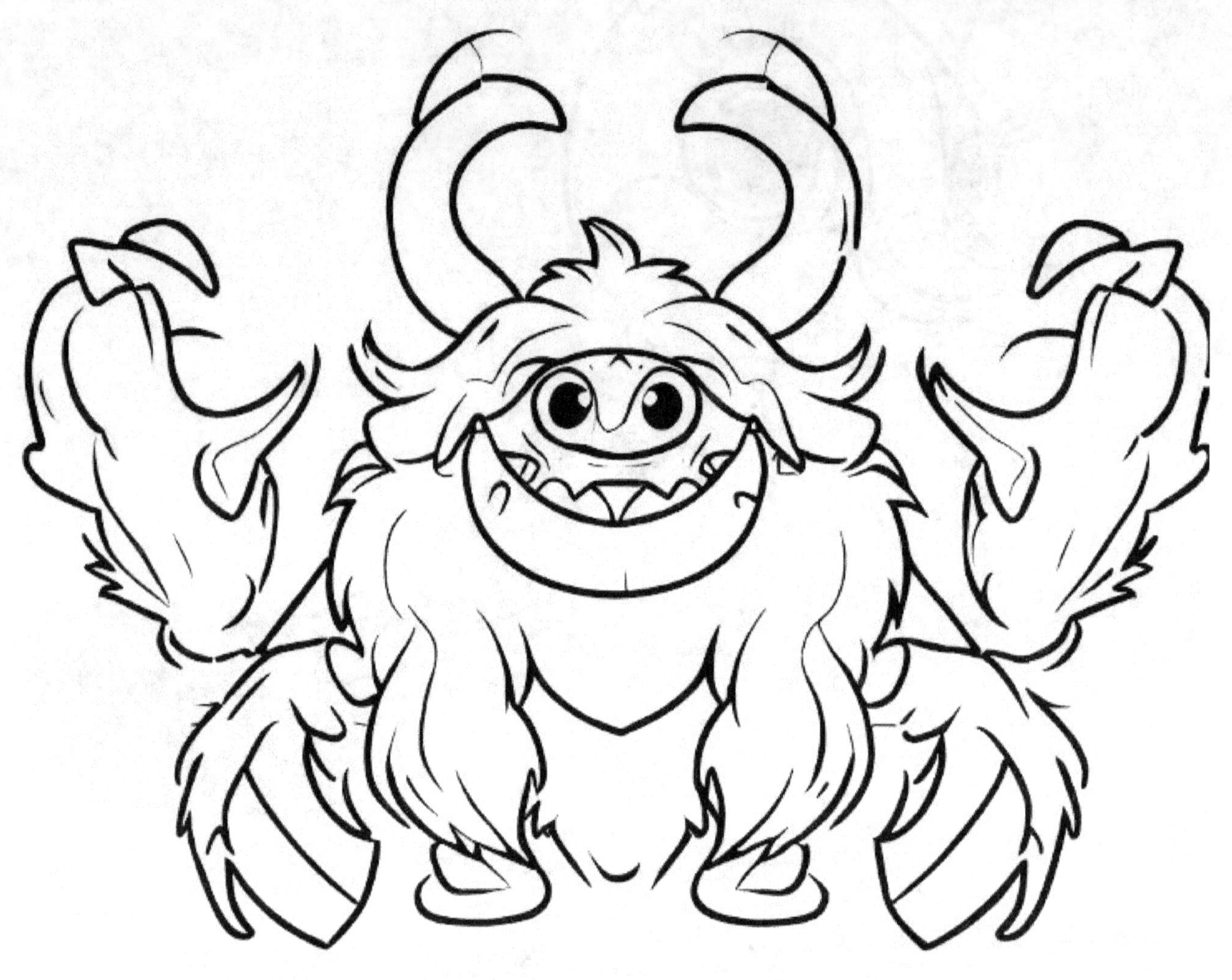

Yeti crab

www.ingramcontent.com/pod-product-compliance
Lightning Source LLC
Chambersburg PA
CBHW080944260726
48661CB00010B/4086